THE STOP

SORIKA

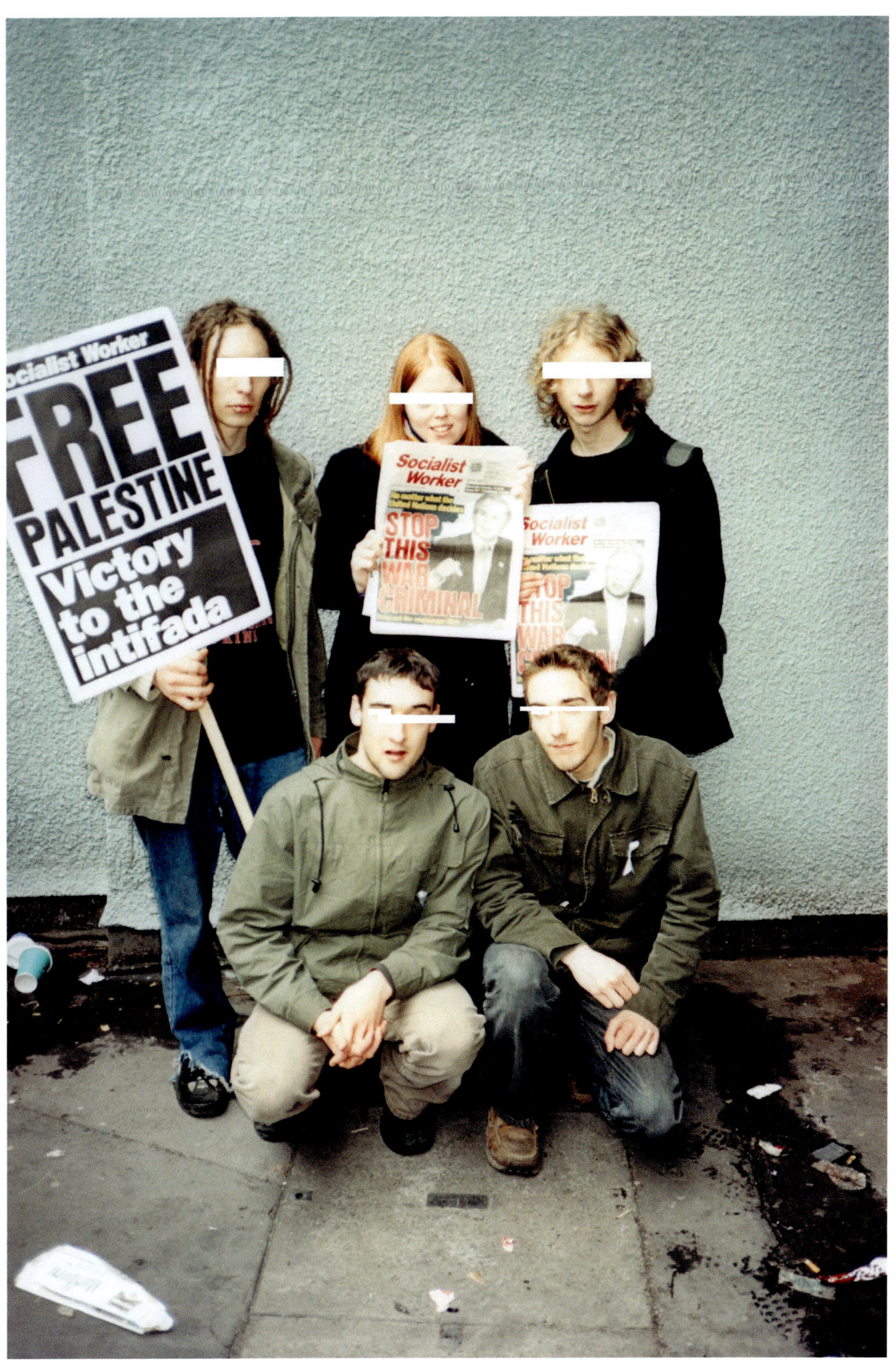
Socialist Worker
FREE
PALESTINE
Victory
to the
intifada
Socialist
Worker
STOP
THIS
WAR
CRIMINAL
Socialist
Worker
STOP
THIS
WAR

The mnemonic of the moment was **WMD**. You hear it
every morning in the news, and every evening in the
pub dick-joked into *Weapons of Mass Dickstruction.*

Then, after a decade or so, you don't hear it anymore.
In the news it is replaced by **jihad**, or **Islamist**, and
sometimes only Arab. And no one goes to the pub how
they used to. Your local's just not your local anymore,
is it?

> VOICEOVER
> *Preparations from first light*
>
> *Silhouetted **officers** patrol*
> *empty cordoned-off streets*
>
> VOICEOVER
> *In the frosty air early morning,*
> ***political** warm-up acts*
>
> On the steps of Whitehall
> a man strums an acoustic guitar
>
> SINGING
> *Peace, peace, **peace**, peace,*
> *let's start talkin' peace*

The important thing about this **mnoronic** moment,
this 15 February 2003, is that it was (yet another)
End of Something and *Beginning of Something
Else.* It was neither *The Very End* nor *An Absolute
Beginning.* It was **mid-pivo**t. Maybe the **epicentre**
of the spin. The "About, face!" Or maybe it had
already started its **reverse** spin-out, building up a
headscarf of steam for *This Exact Moment*, now,
or *The Next Moment Yet* (always hard to tell, when
you're in *The Moment*, which exact moment it is).

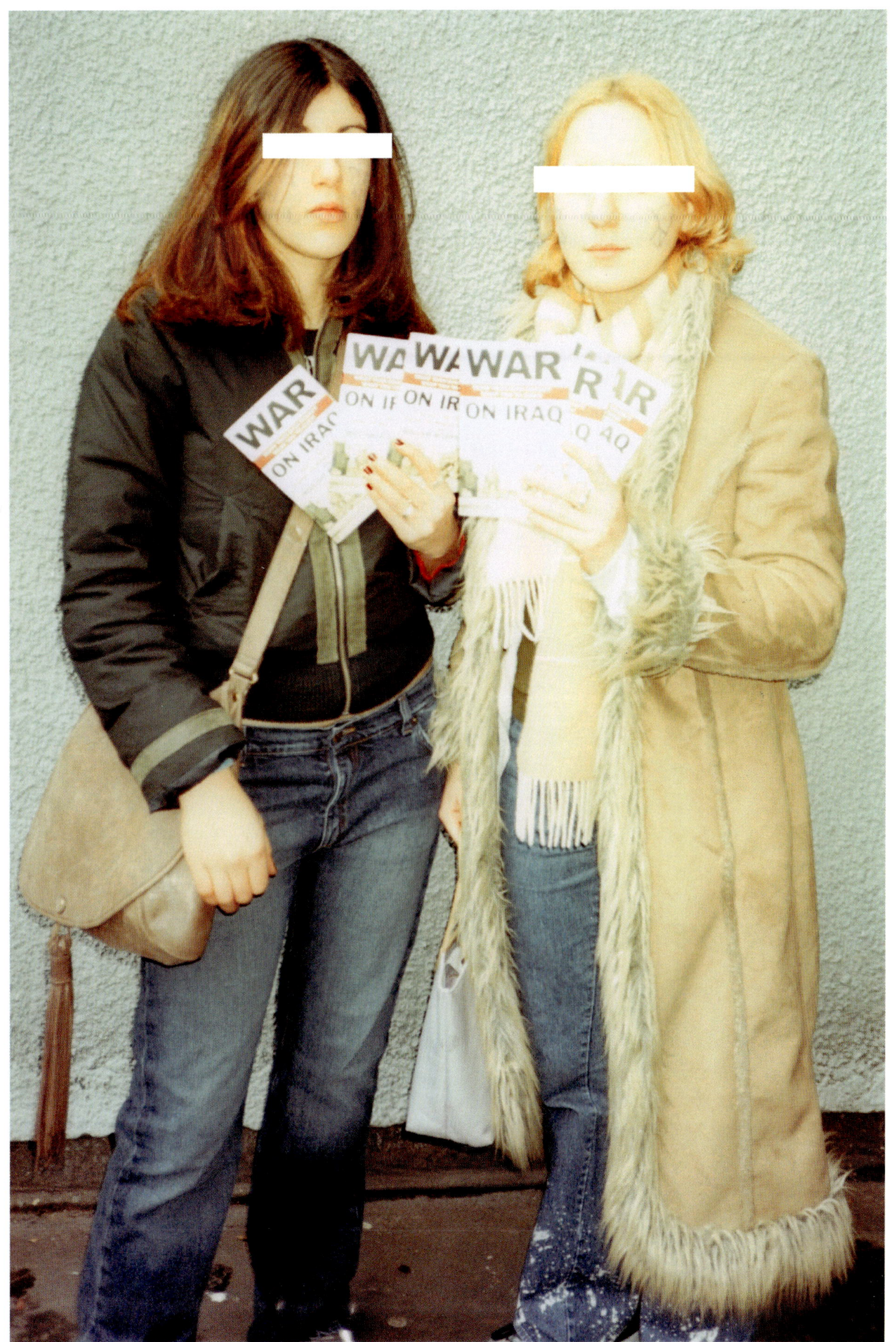

WAR ON IRAQ
WAR ON IRAQ
WAR ON IRAQ
WAR ON IRAQ

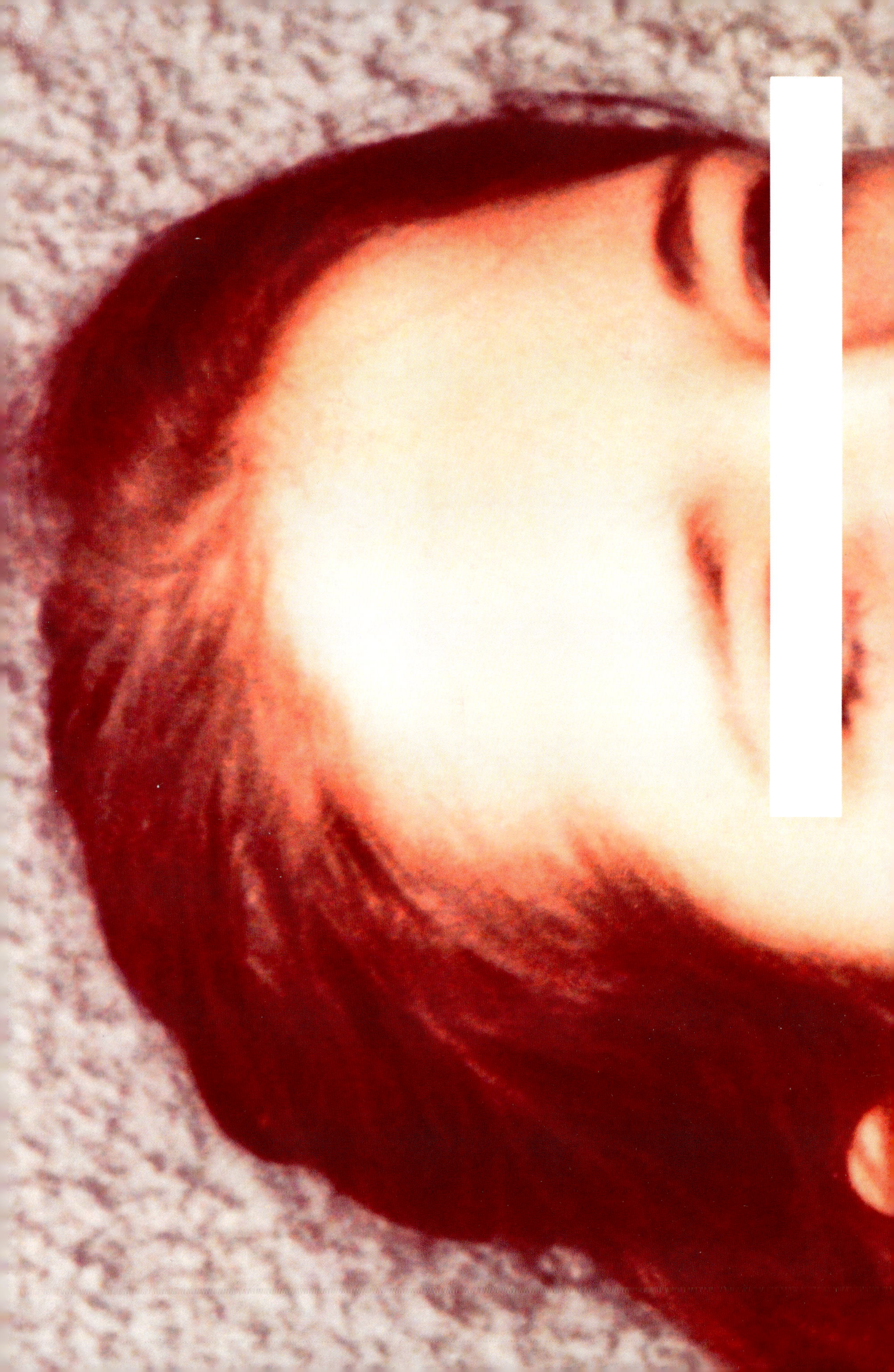

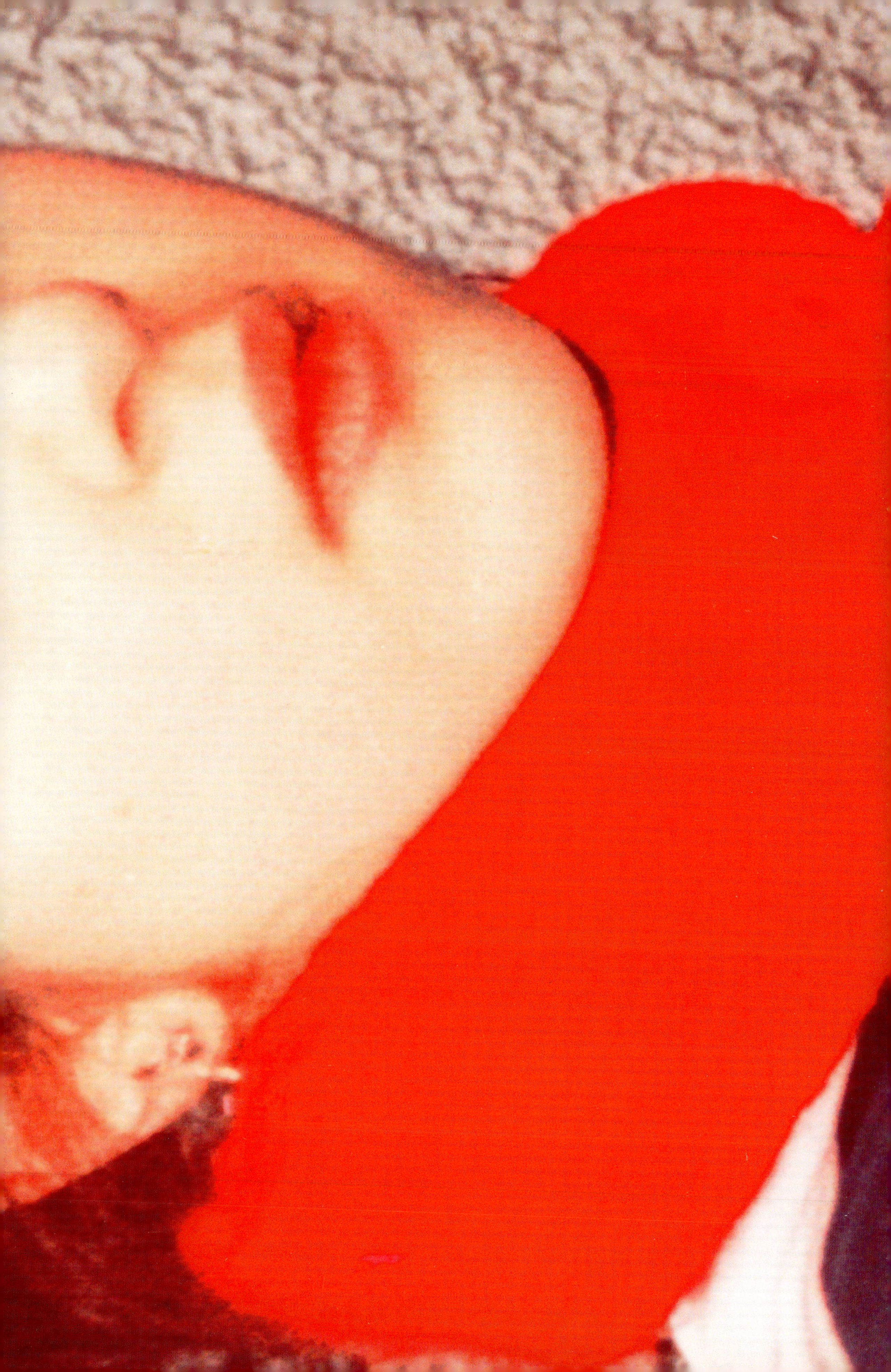

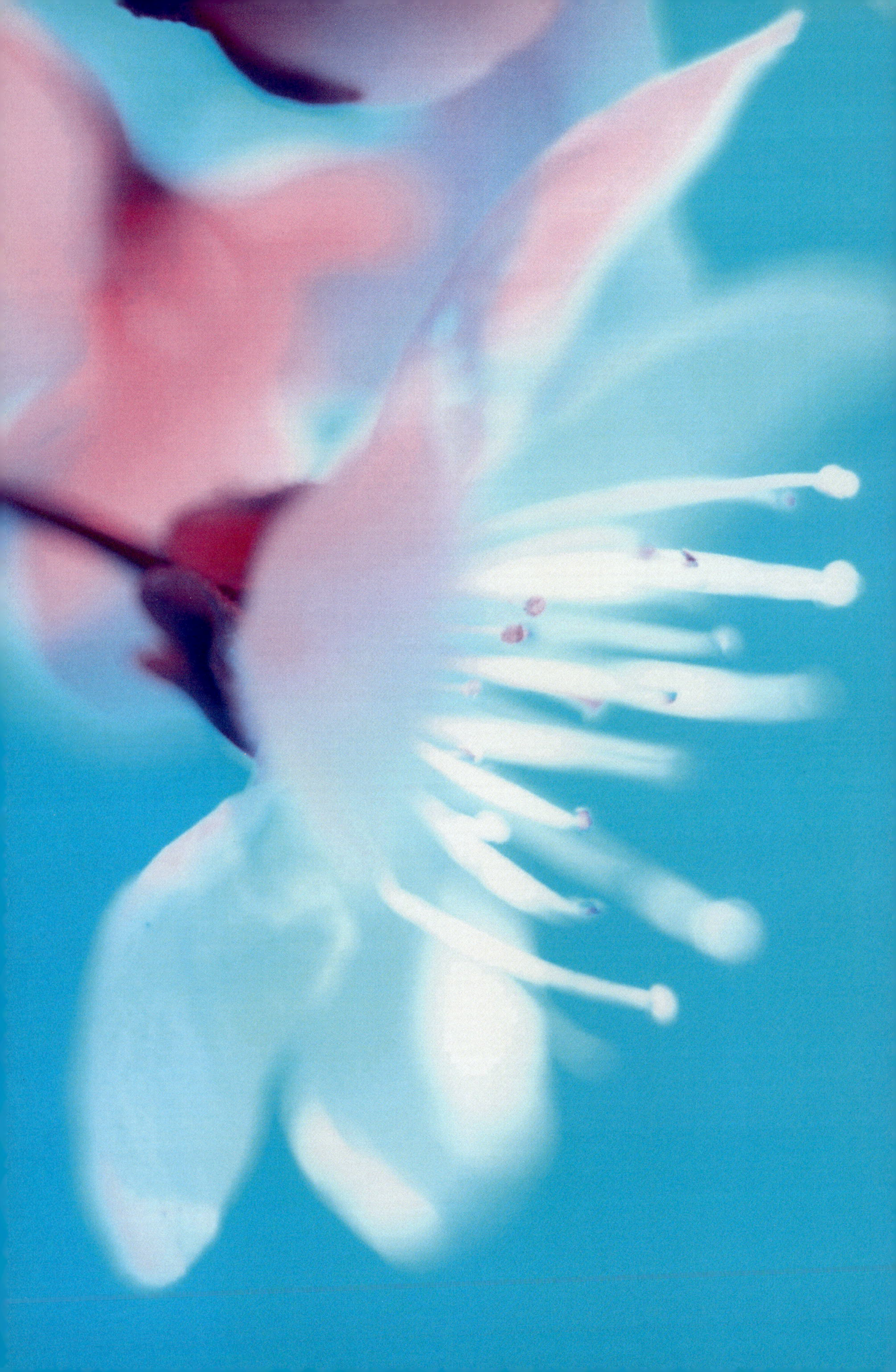

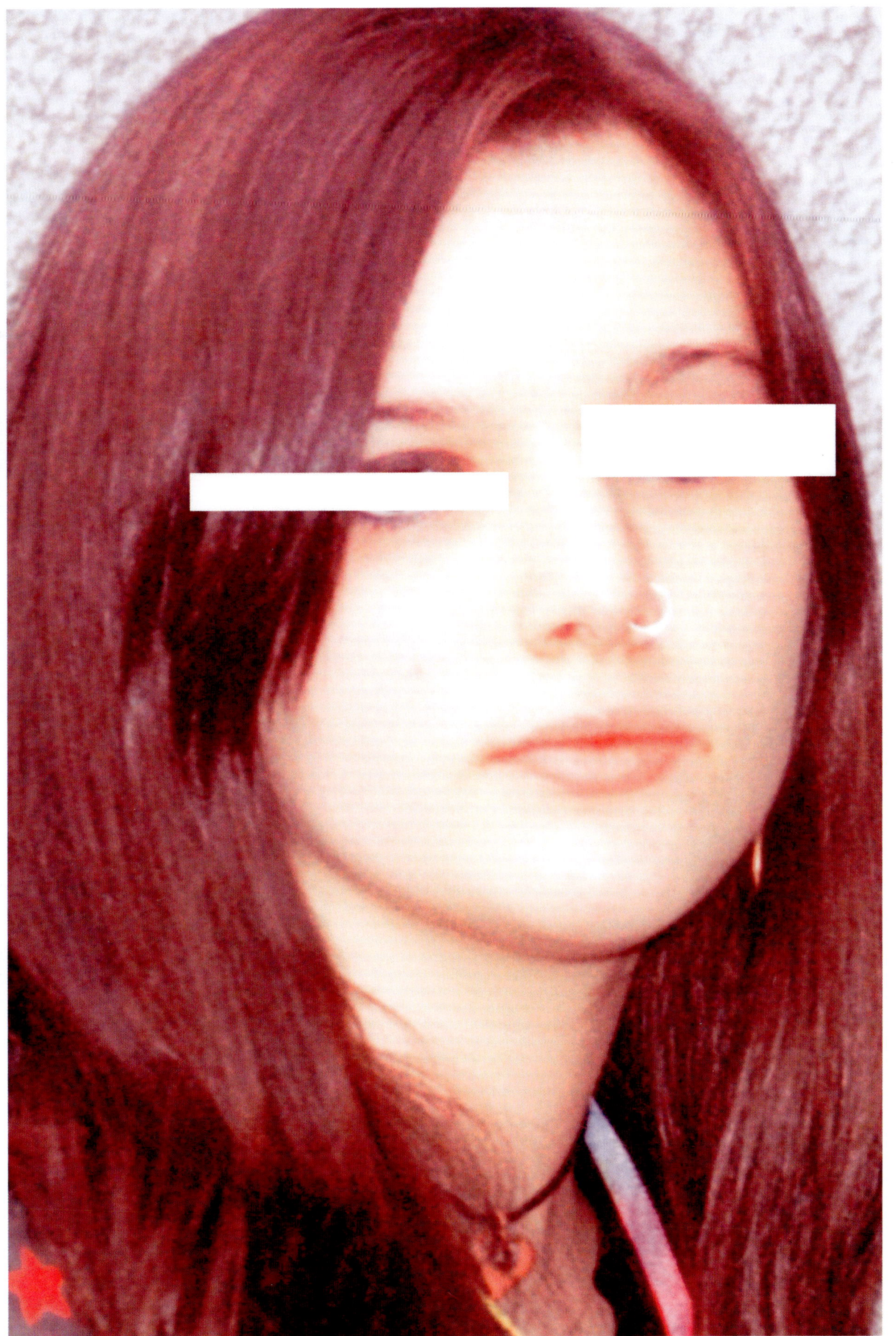

Wide aerial shot of march
People *dressed as British Prime*
Minister Tony Blair and US President
*George W. Bush **kissing***

VOICEOVER
Hundreds of coaches booked.
Chartered trains from across
the country

SOUNDBITE
Even though United are playing
I think it's probably better to come
to London because it's to try and
stop the war.

After 9/11.

Before *The Internet*.

And before mobile phones. (Both had breached the
military industrial complex and been birthed into the
society but they haven't yet hybred into the *Weapons
of Mass Distraction* they will become.)

VOICEOVER
This was Hyde Park, The Strand,
Embankment

Tilt down from **neon advertising**
to man conducting choir

Choir singing

Banners in march

VOICEOVER
Where're you from?

SOUNDBITE
Sheffield

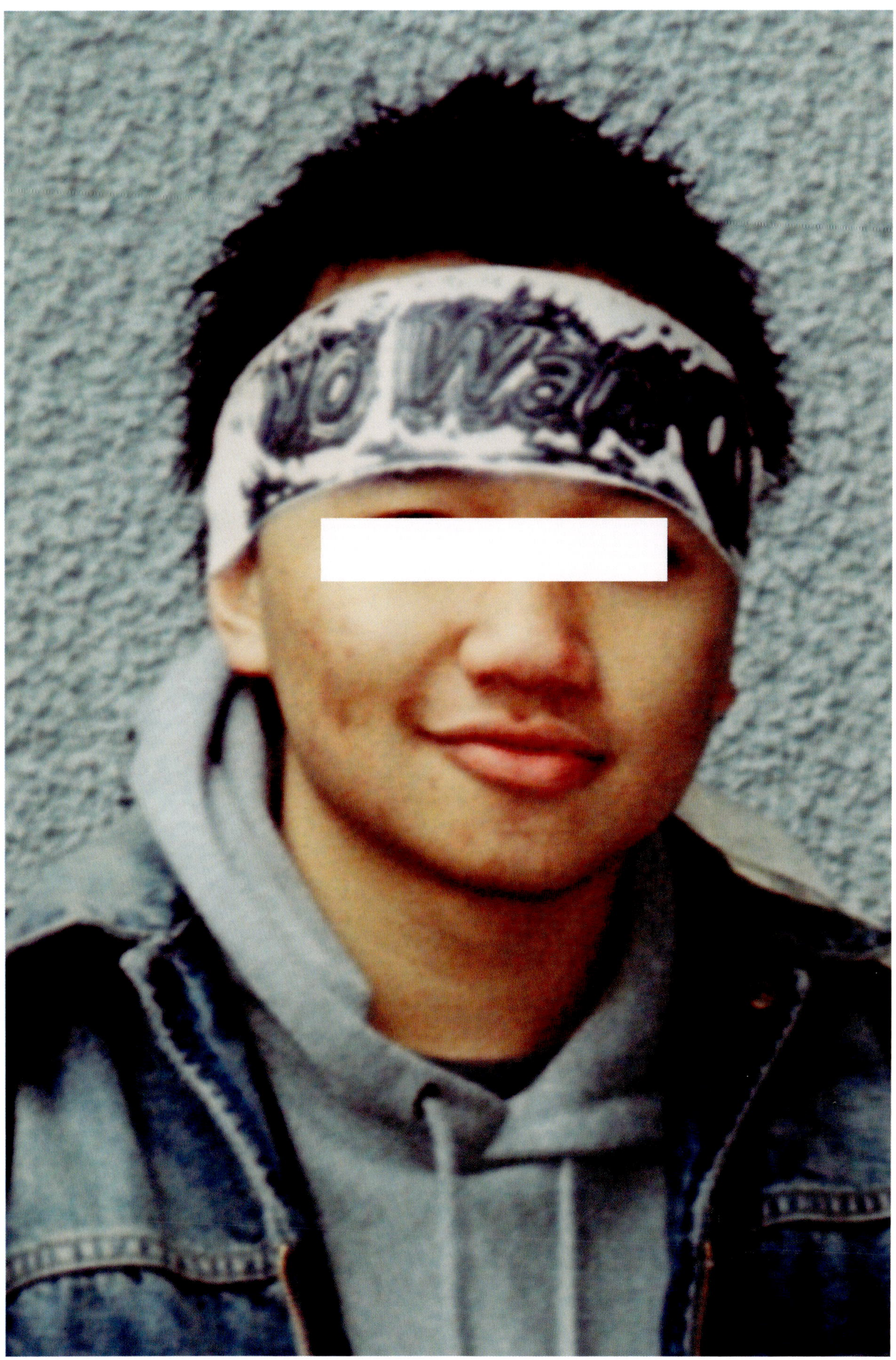
No War

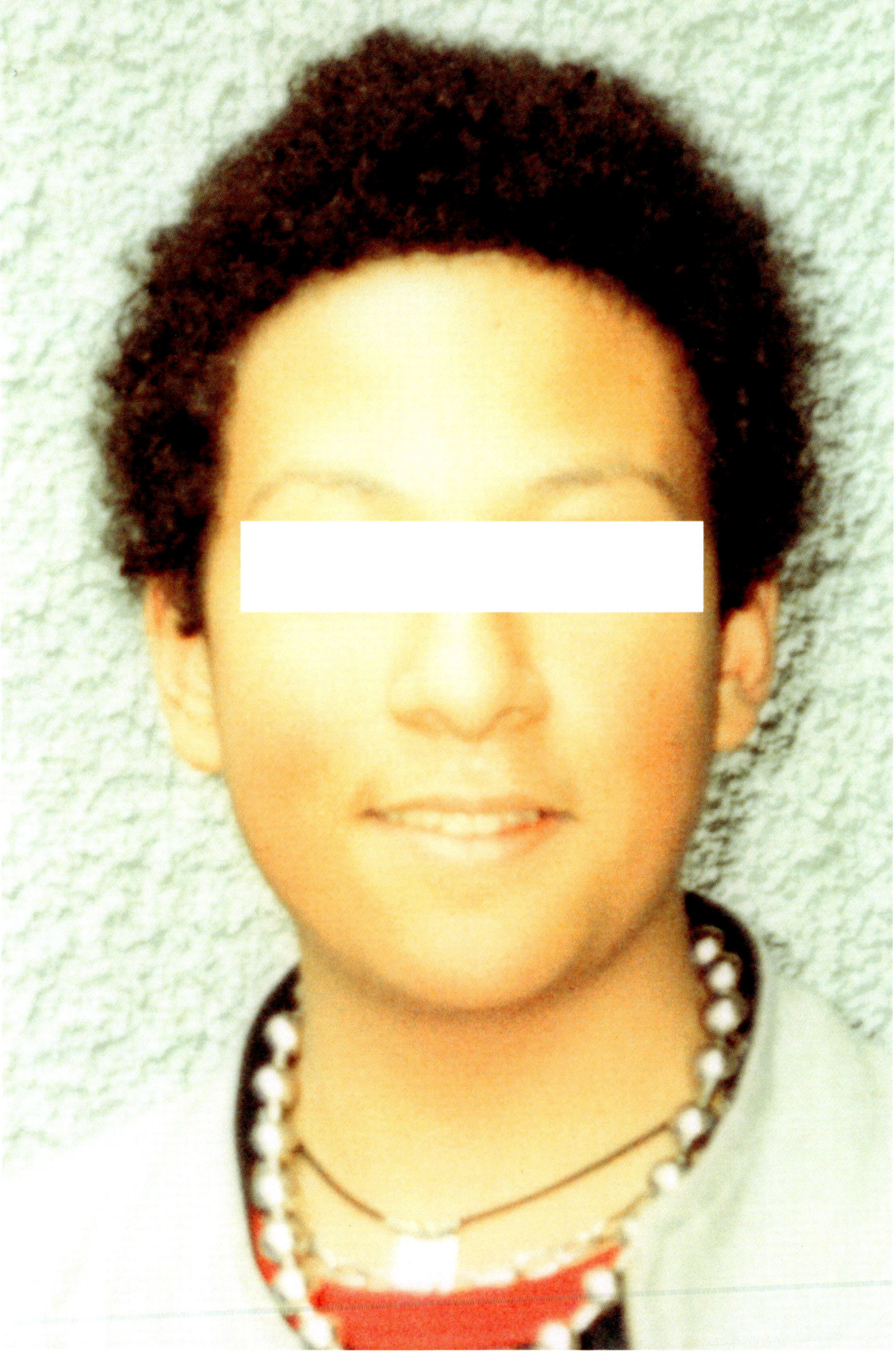

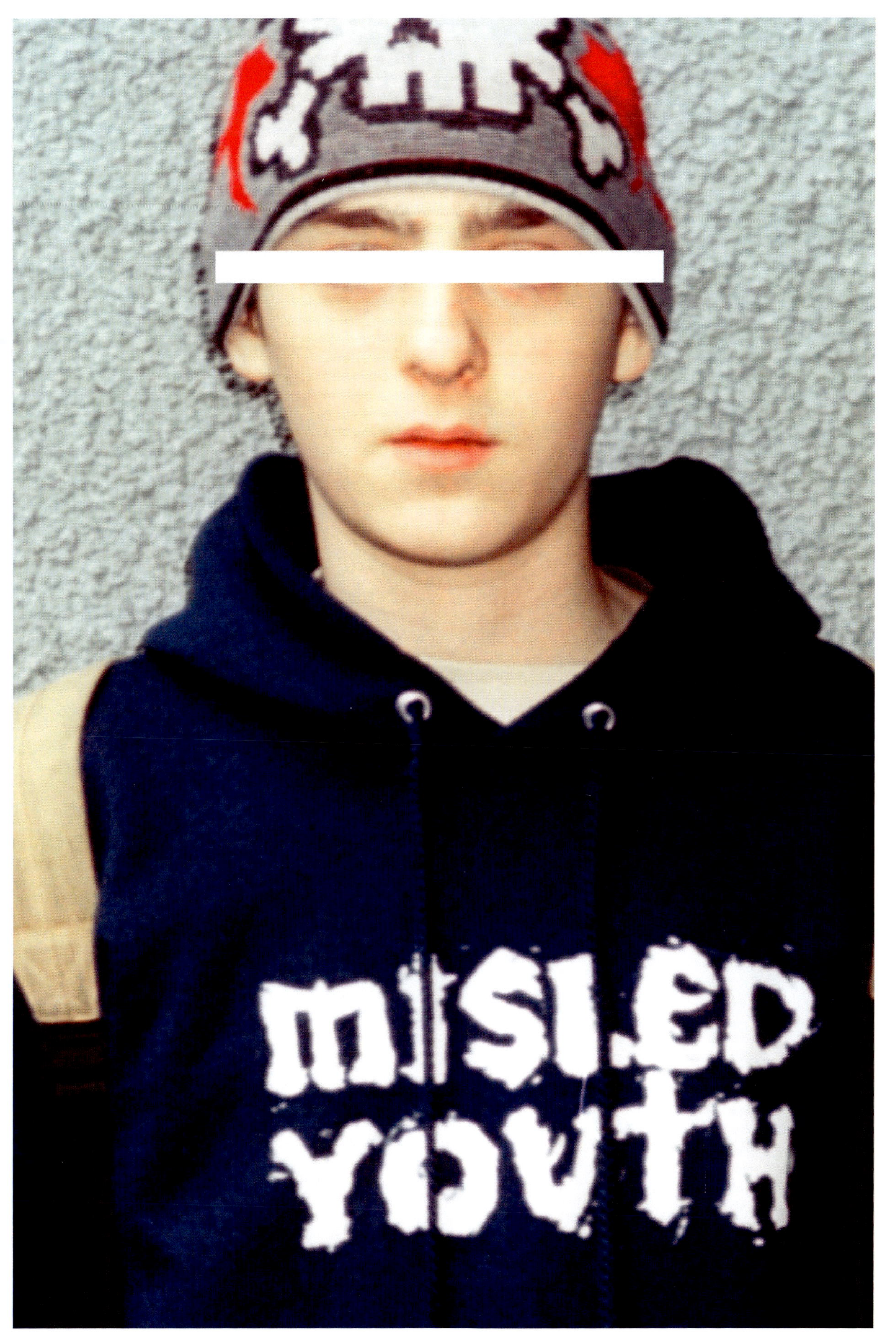
misled
youth

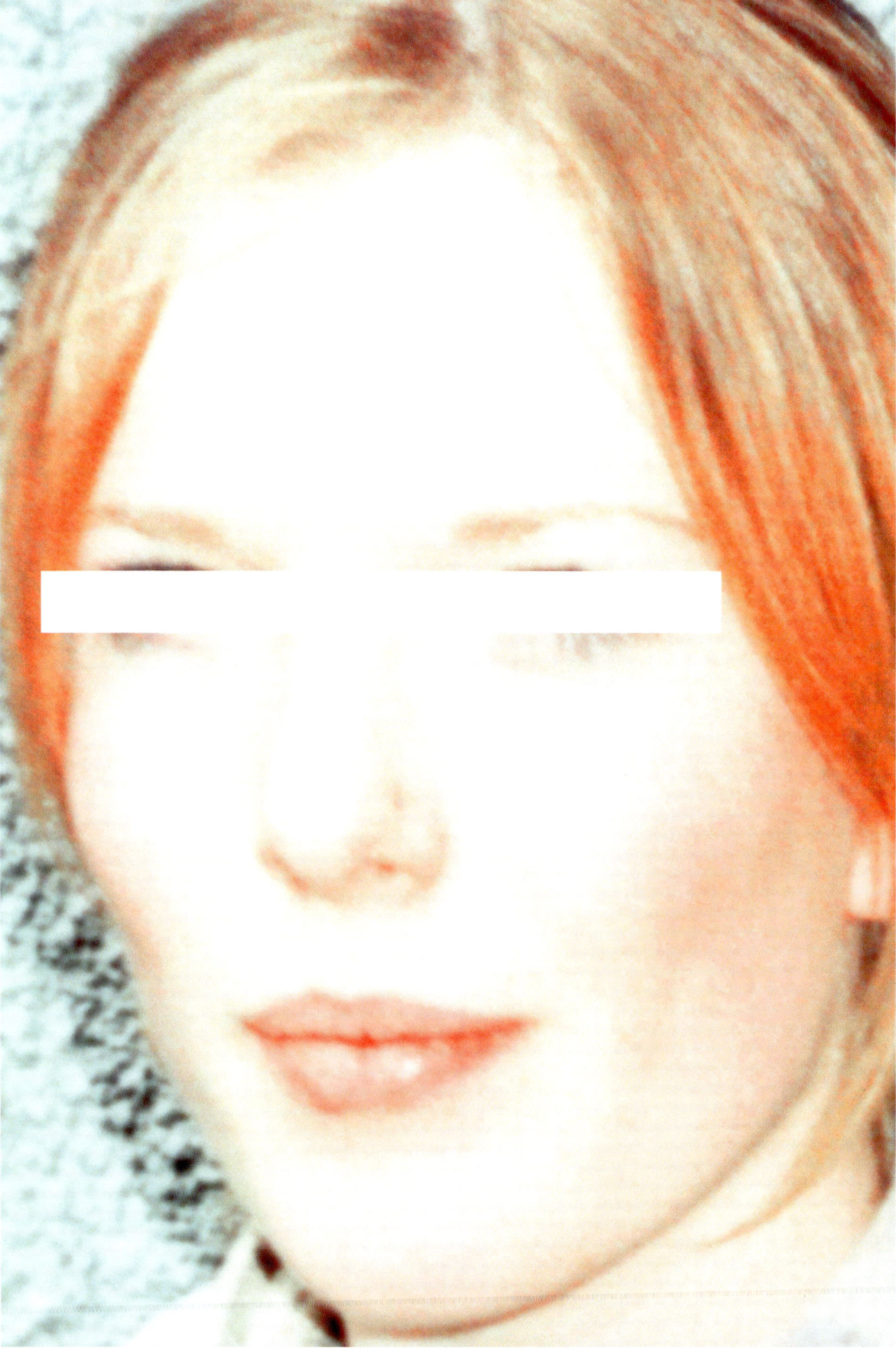

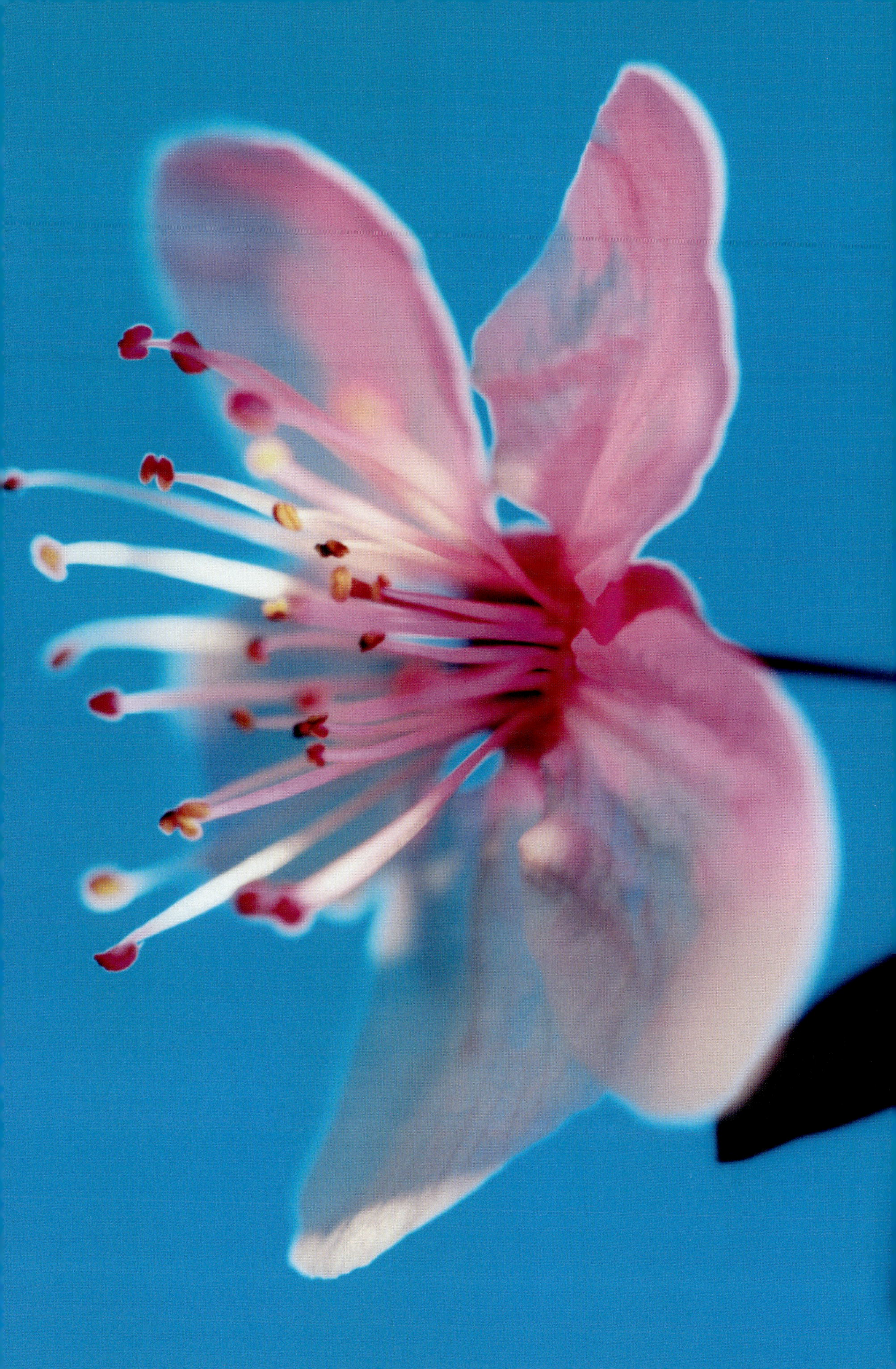

SOUNDBITE
Leeds

SOUNDBITE
Suffolk

SOUNDBITE
Barnsley

SOUNDBITE
Birmingham

SOUNDBITE
London

SOUNDBITE
From Bedford

SOUNDBITE
From Cumbria

SOUNDBITE
London, Stoke Newington

SOUNDBITE
From Banbury

SOUNDBITE
from Edinburgh

SOUNDBITE
Northamptonshire

SOUNDBITE
from Malaysia

SOUNDBITE
North Wales

SOUNDBITE
Sheffield

SOUNDBITE
Birmingham

SOUNDBITE
*Yeah, I come from Bristol, **man***

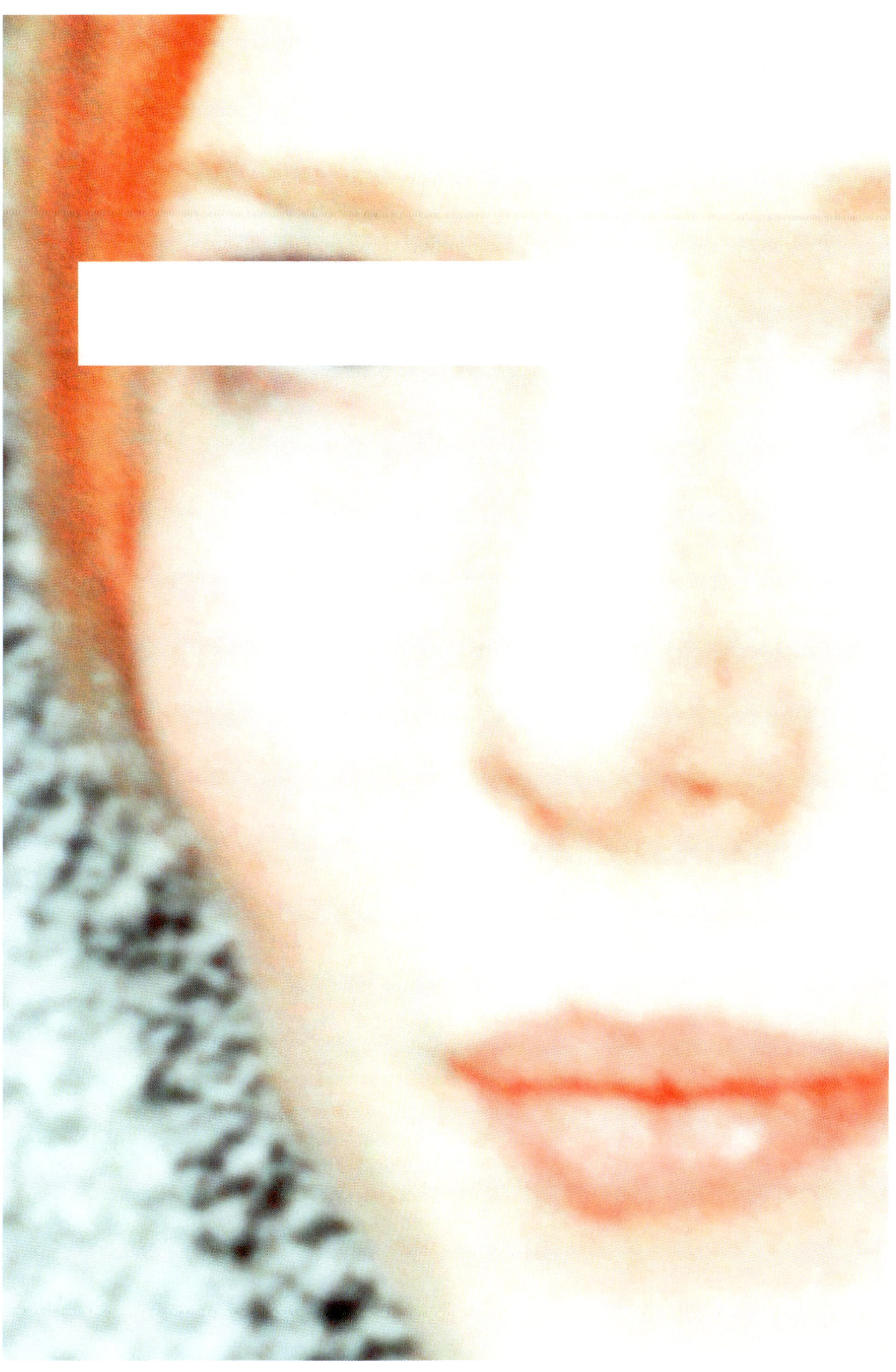

There are no messaging **apps**. There is no social
media, not any that can accompany you through
the streets, notificationing, anyway.

People send text messages on their phones. They
play **Snake** on their phones. They make images out
of **punctuation marks** (the most fun) on their phones.

> VOICEOVER
> *Celebrity campaigners are out of bed*
> *and out in force*
>
> SOUNDBITE
> *This is a historical day. A day to,*
> *um, remember!*
>
> SHOUTING
> *B-Liar! B-Liar! Pants on fire!*
>
> VOICEOVER
> *Thousands from the east, from the*
> *west, from the north and the south.*
>
> *Faces hidden behind banners*
> *and pre-fab Socialist Worker placards*
>
> VOICEOVER
> *From the left, from the right, from the*
> *radical, from the uncommitted:*
> *they came.*

Now it's a norm to complain about how **shit**
phones and social media are. **Complaints** include
(1) unsolicited content, (2) constant availability,
(3) privacy, (4) annoyingness, (5) sinister. But **anti-
socials** sentiment is always addendumed by a reason
why the talker can't come off of them. Reasons include
(5) a **family** WhatsApp group, (6a and b) how else
to stay abreast of current affairs and the creative
endeavours of **others**, and (7) your service provider
charging to send pictures as texts.

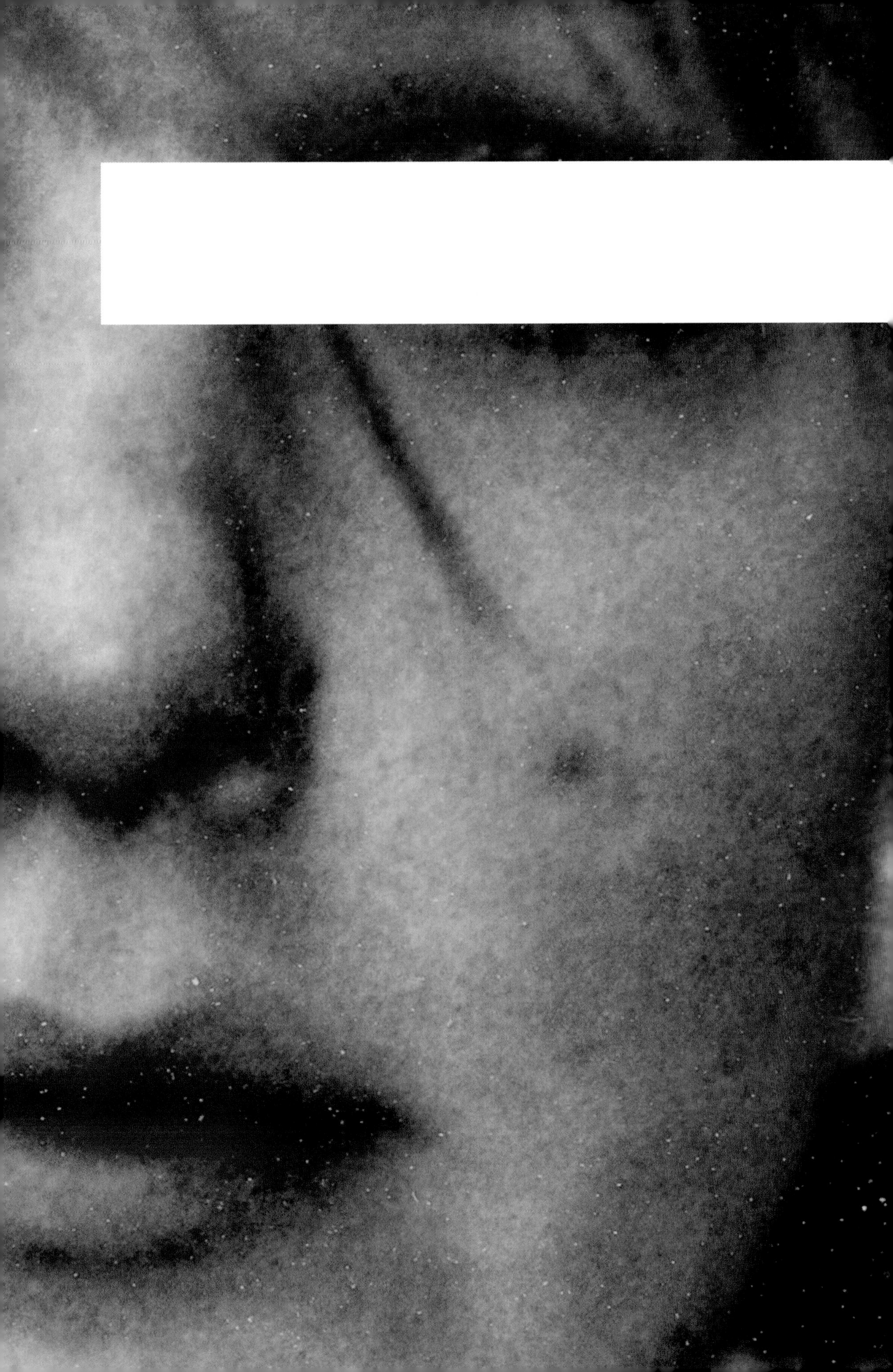

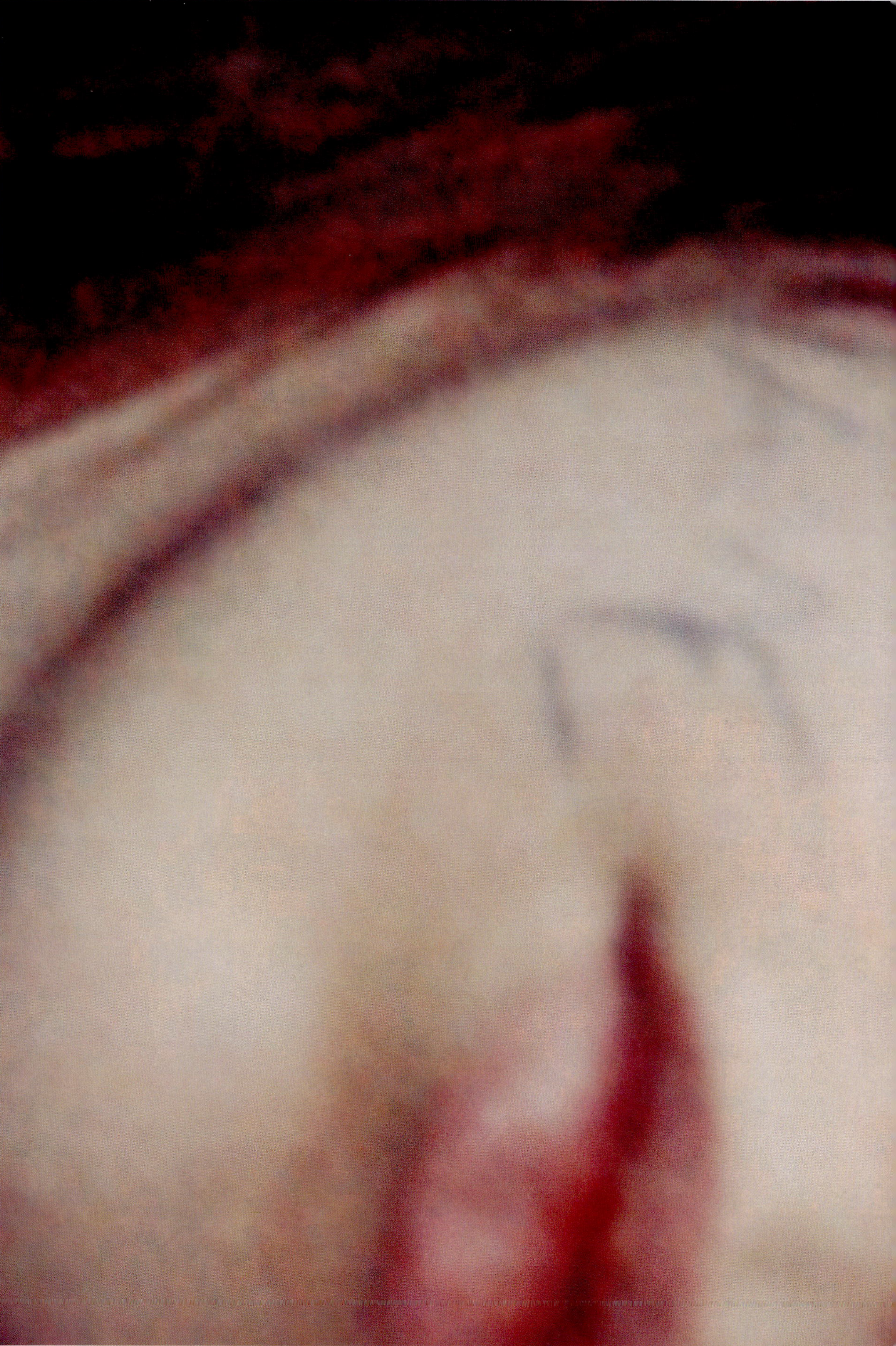

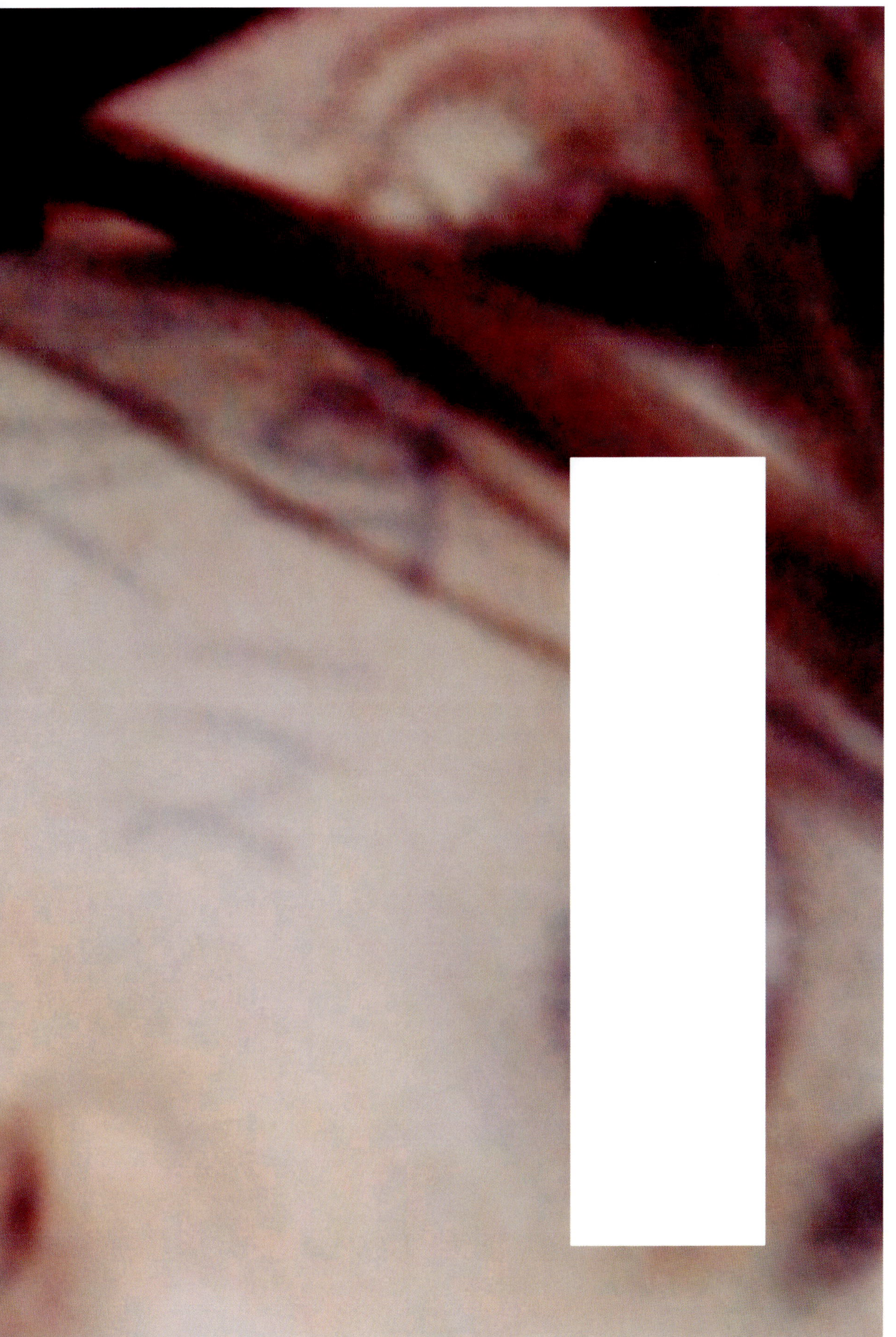

Horses

VOICEOVER
*It was the day the police simply
banished the car from central London*

Child on shoulders in crowd

SOUNDBITE
*I just think the world's going mad.
I just feel it's got to be stopped,
somewhere. Because after this, it'll be
something else. It'll be war after war
after war.*

The notion that it is impossible to organise without the
connectivity phones provide is now near-sacred, but
The Stop (as it is affectionately named by organisers
during the organisational phase), *The Stop* is everything
that phones and social media later promise to deliver
- and instead **destroy**. The **ease** with which people are
able to share their thoughts has, as we all know, not
made it easier to put a cohesive strategy to oppose the
world's more malign agendas in motion. It's done the
exact opposite of that. Now is **genocide** dipped in **rice
water** and honey face mask **reels** and hipster-austerity
gardening-crypto **memes**.

*Pan from protestors dancing to
people playing instruments.*

SOUNDBITE
*I don't want to see any war in the world,
that's why I'm here*

*Wide shot of march with man dancing
on stilts in foreground*

*Pakistani protestors with banner
(Democratic Revolutionary Party)*

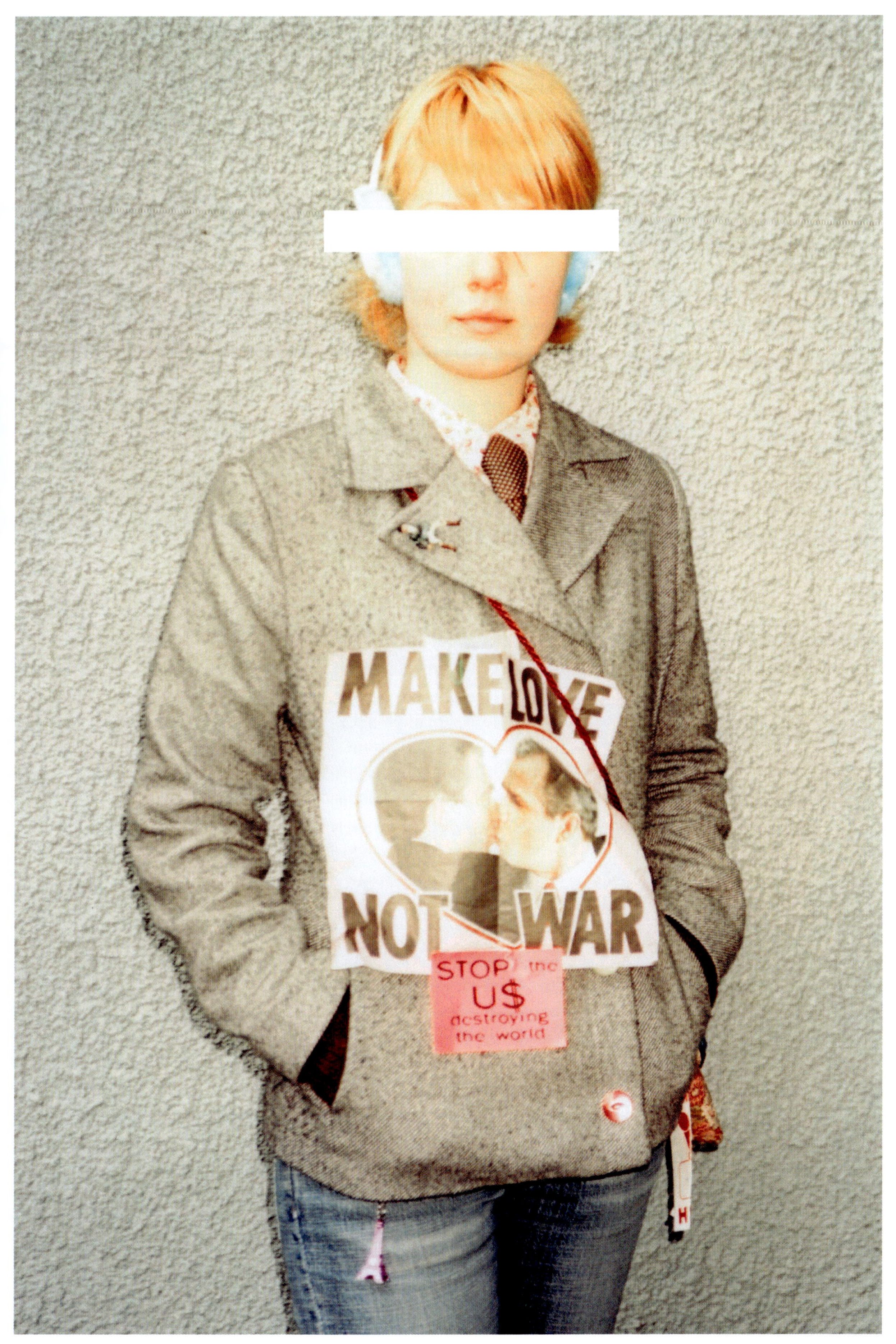

MAKE LOVE
NOT WAR
STOP the
U$
destroying
the world

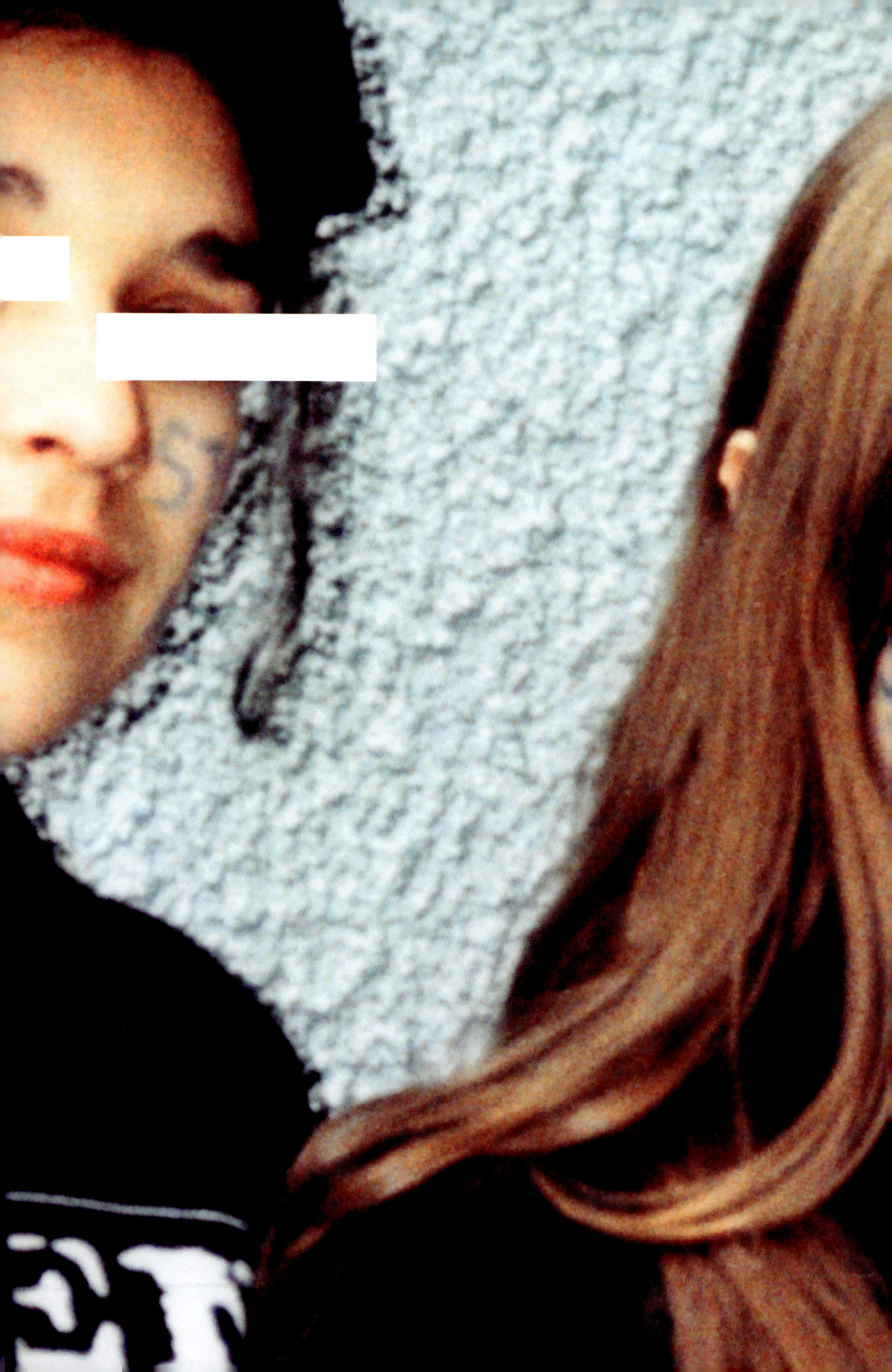

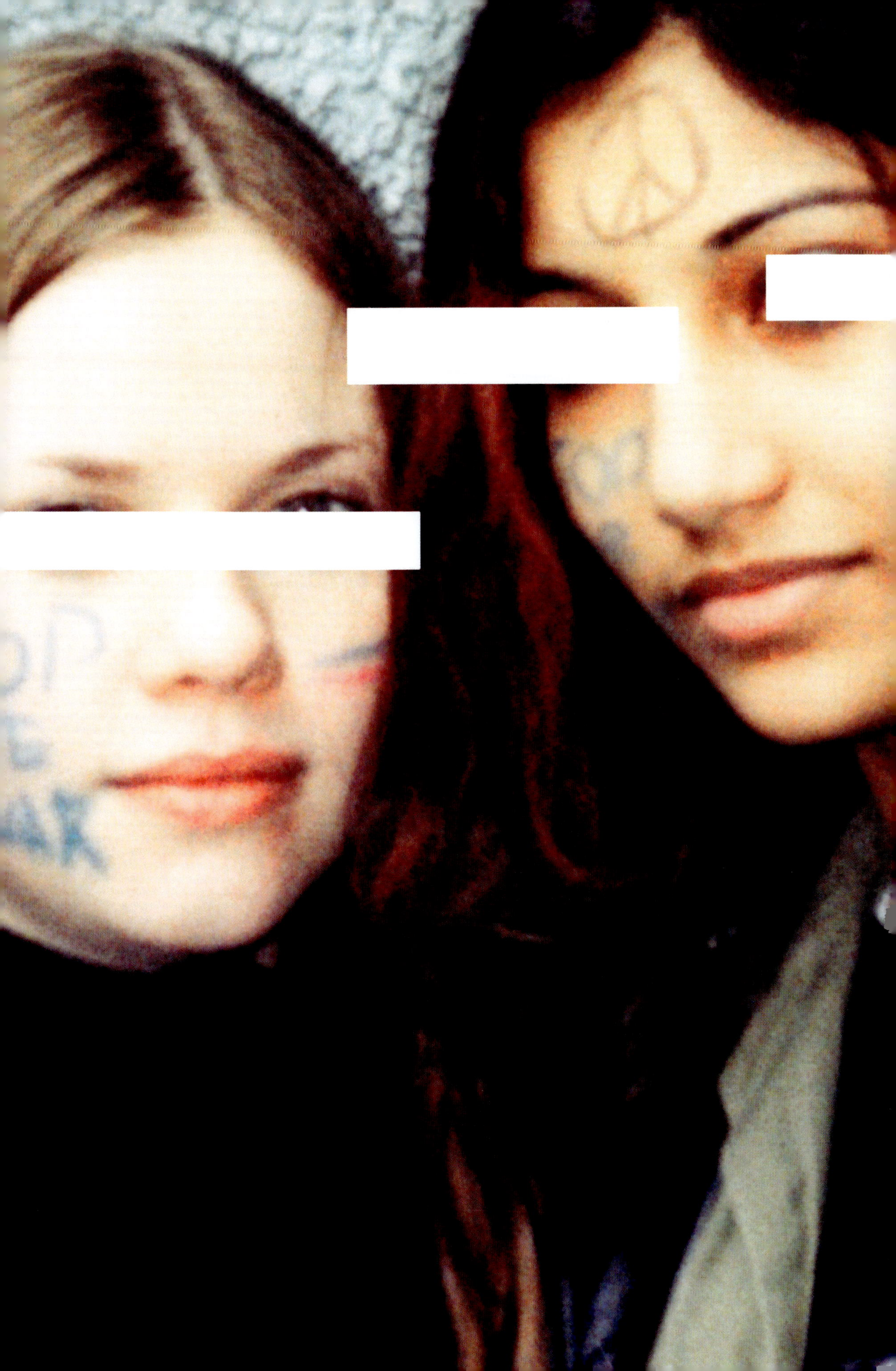

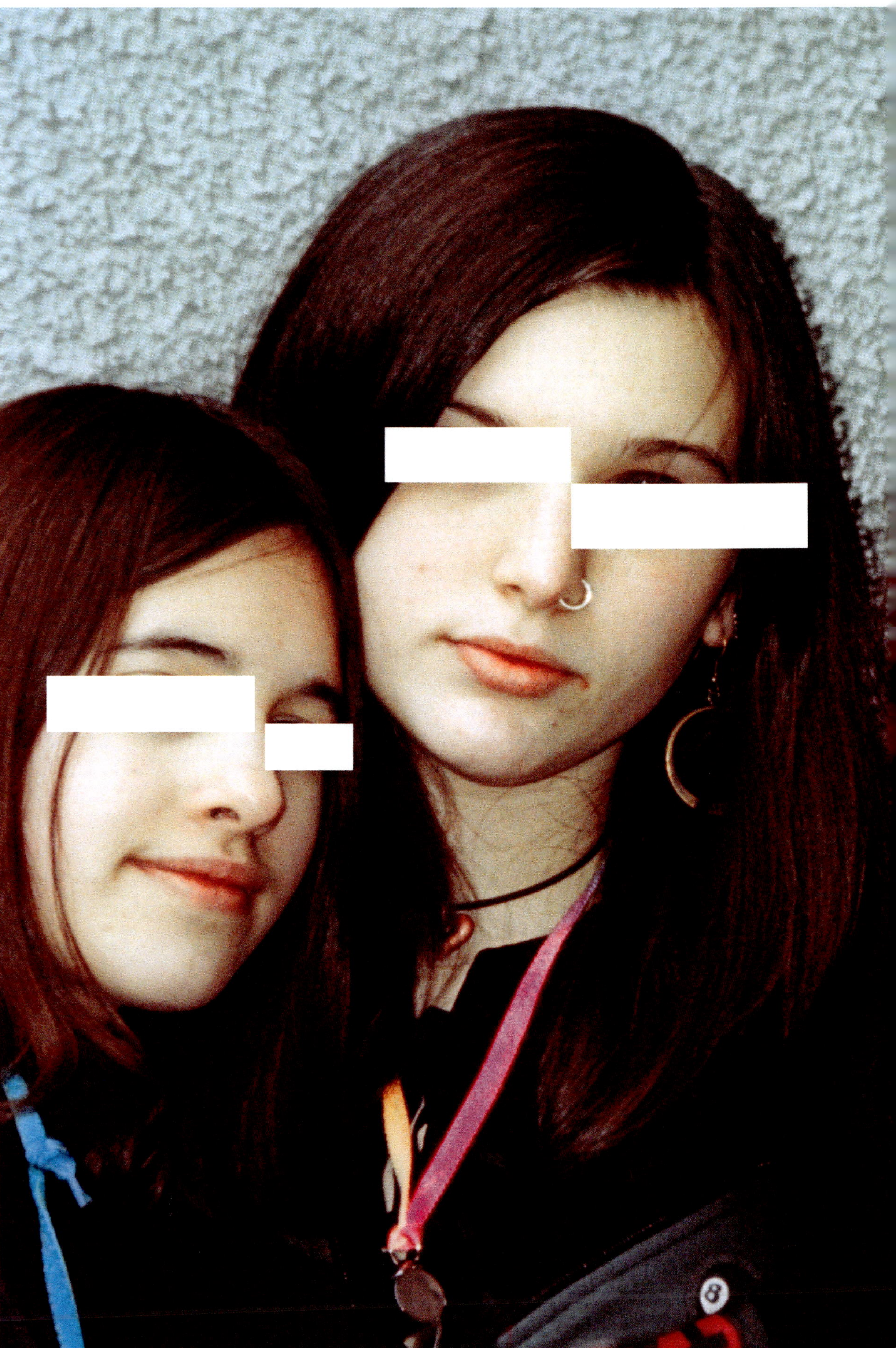

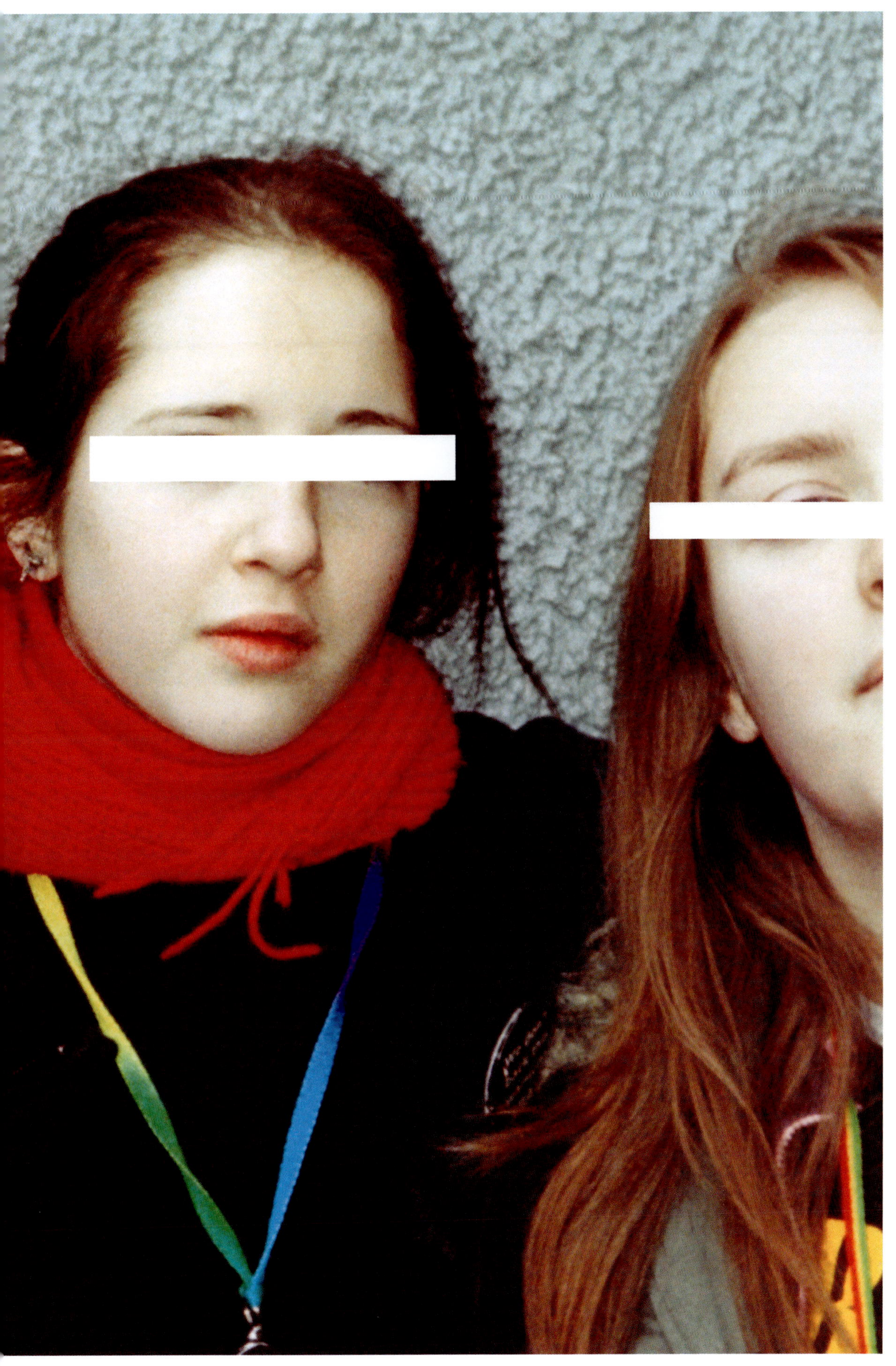

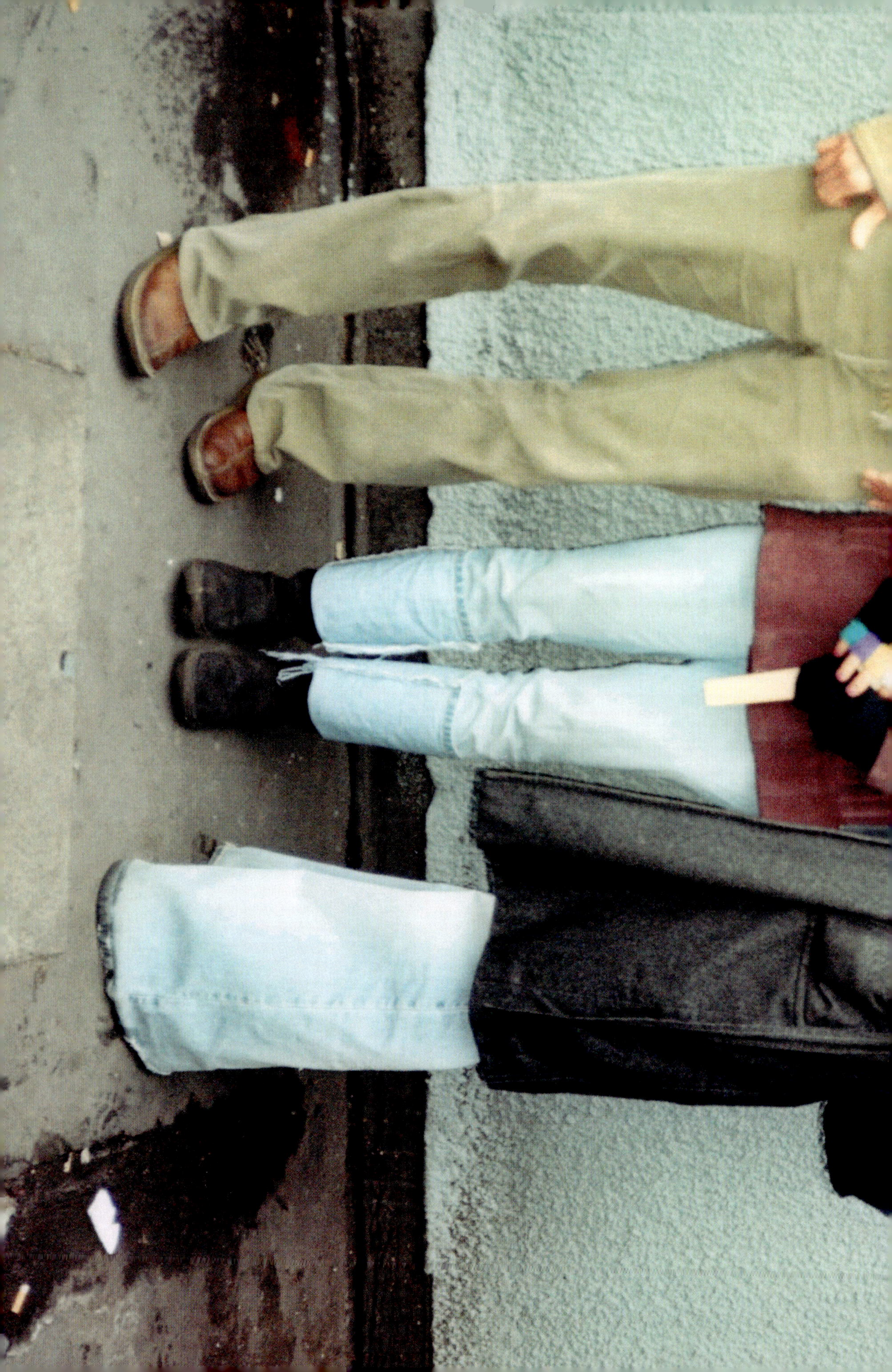

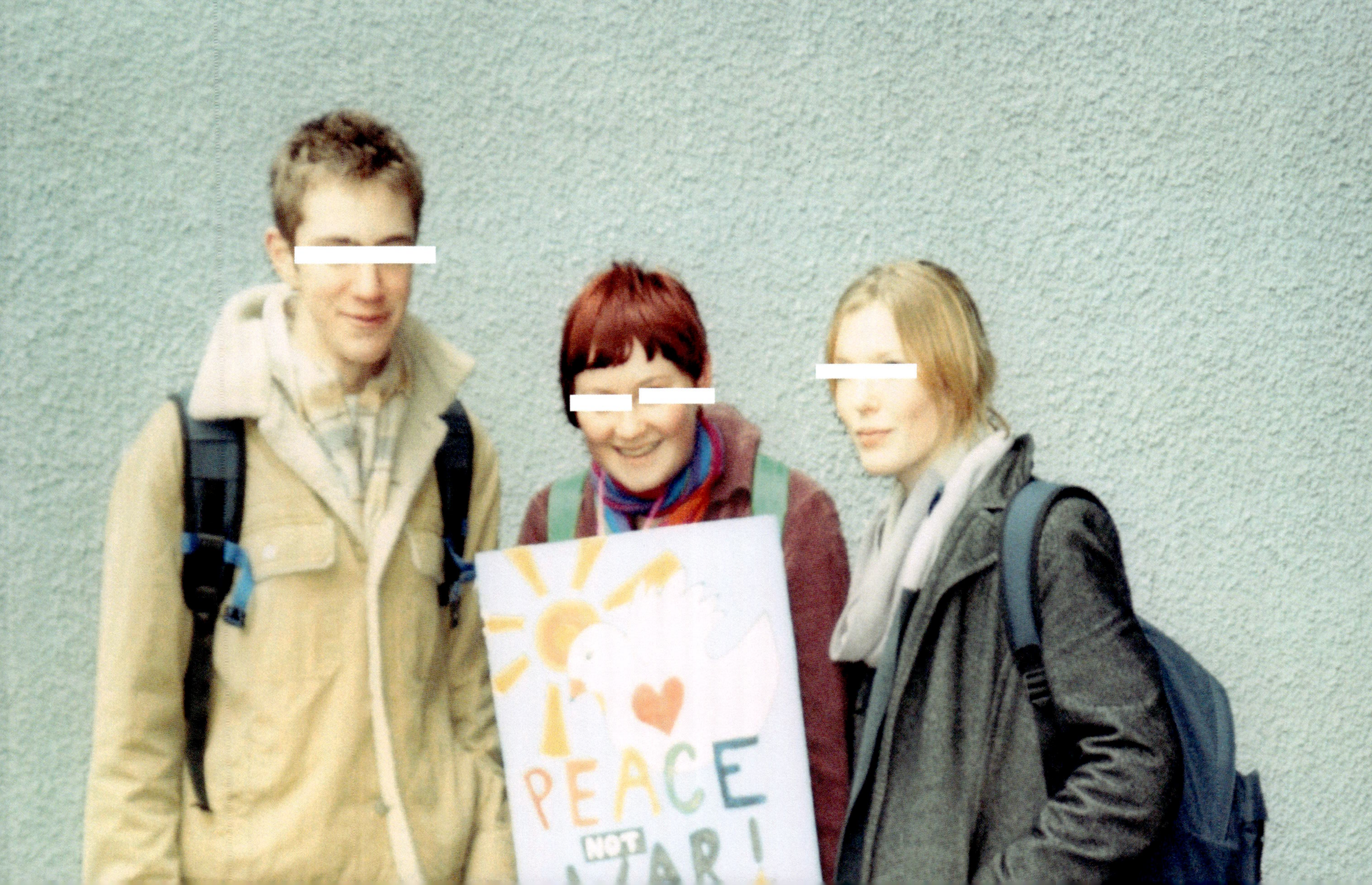
PEACE
NOT
WAR!

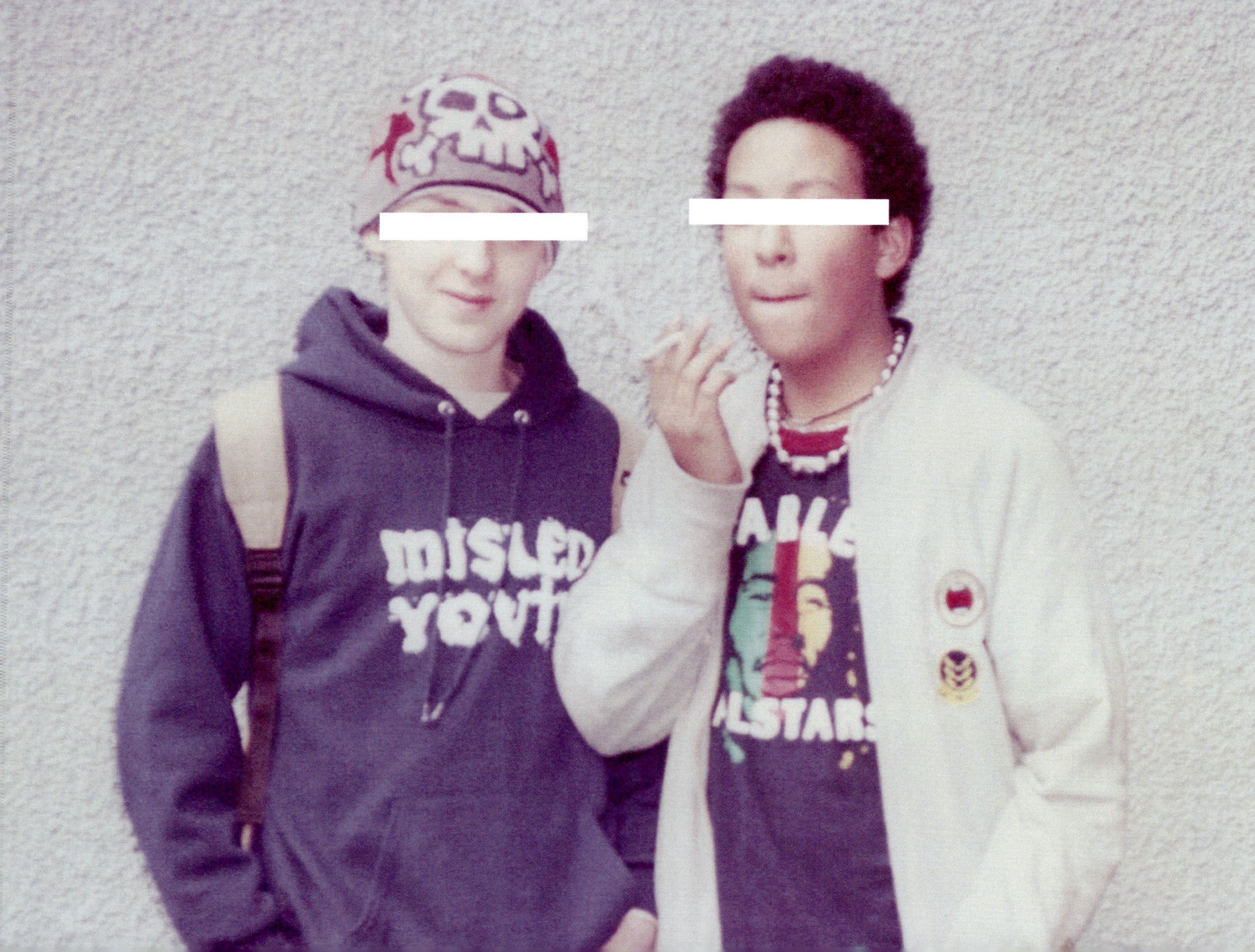
MISLED
YOUTH
ALLG
ALSTARS

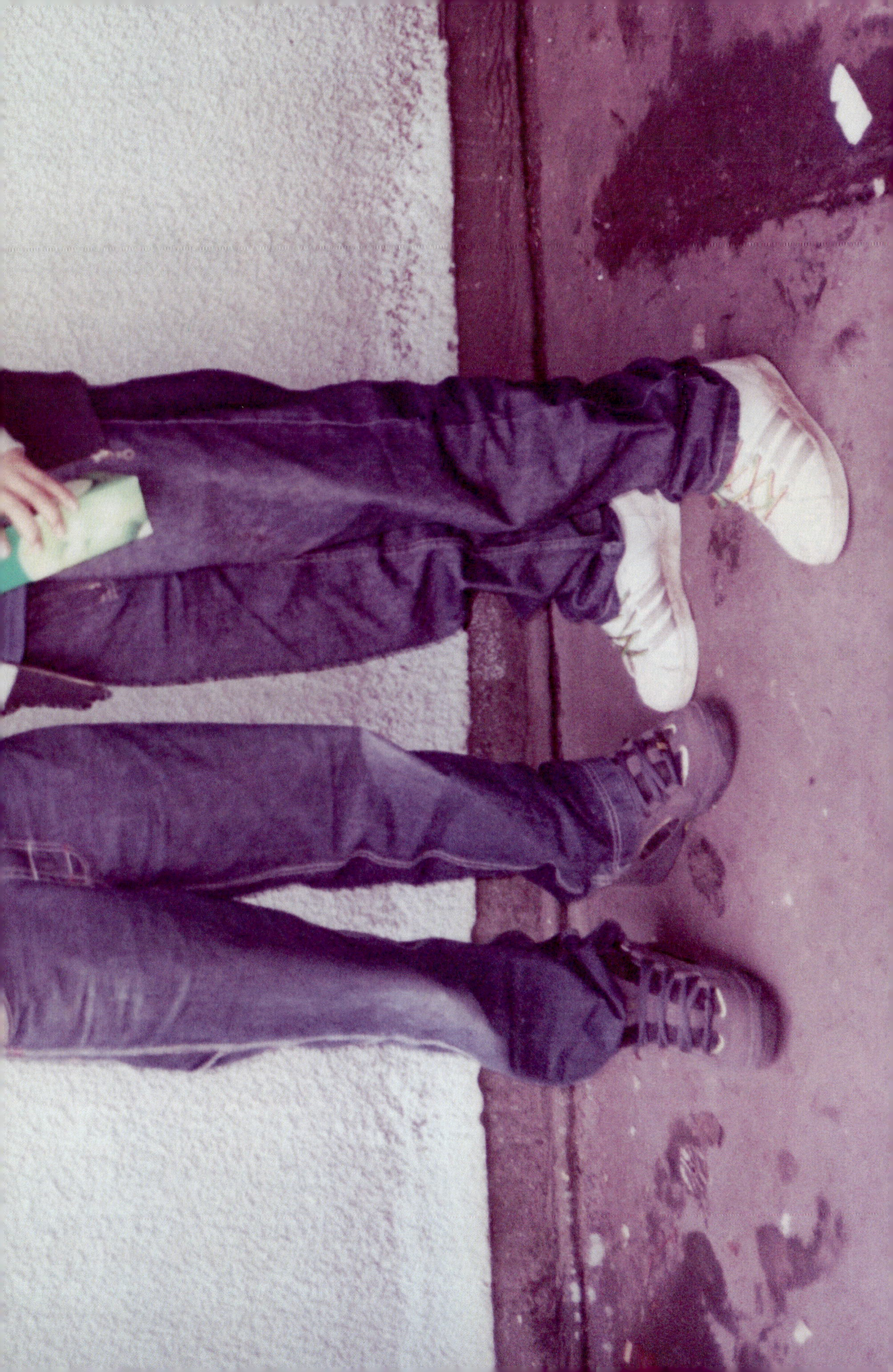

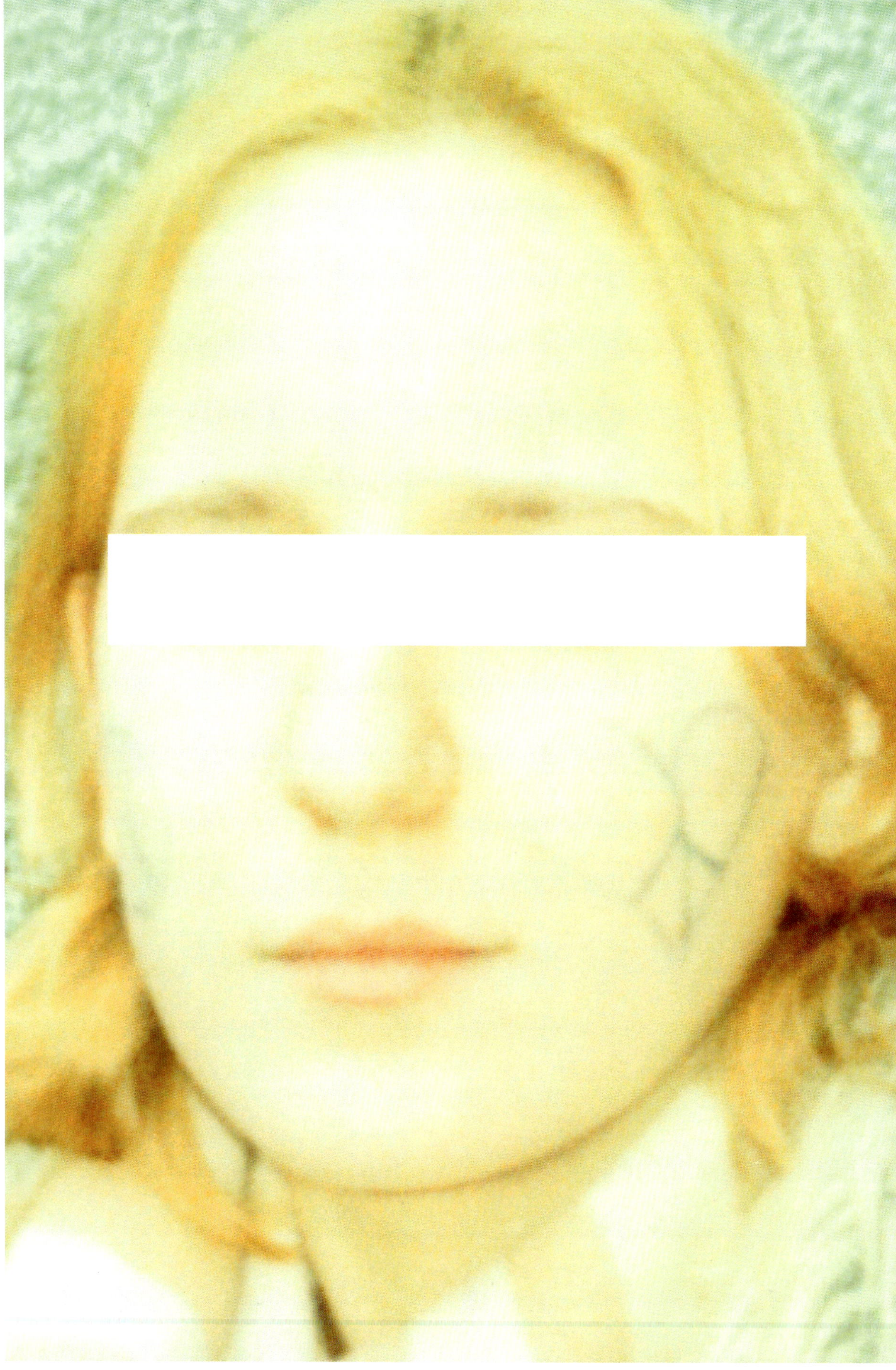

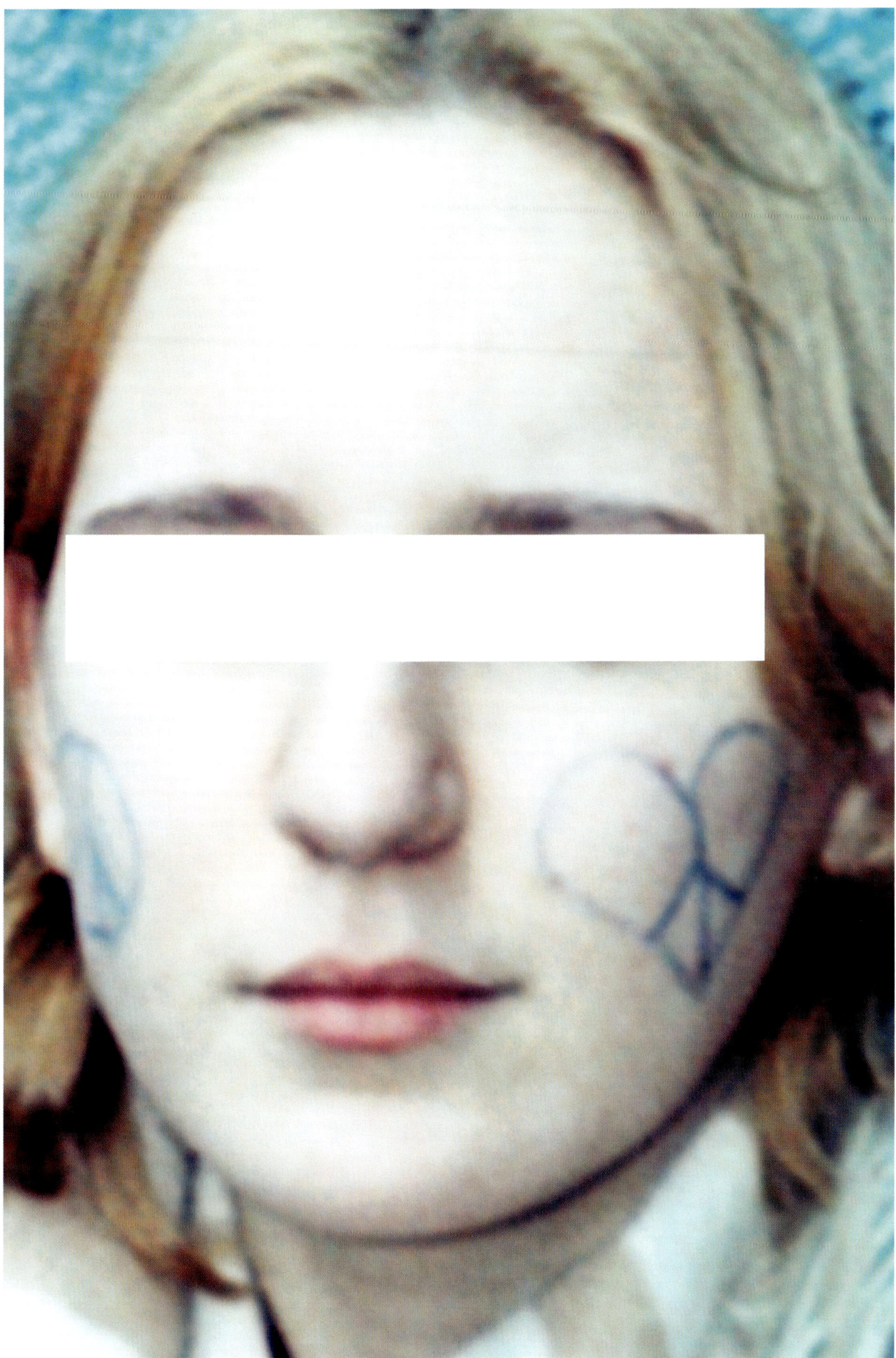

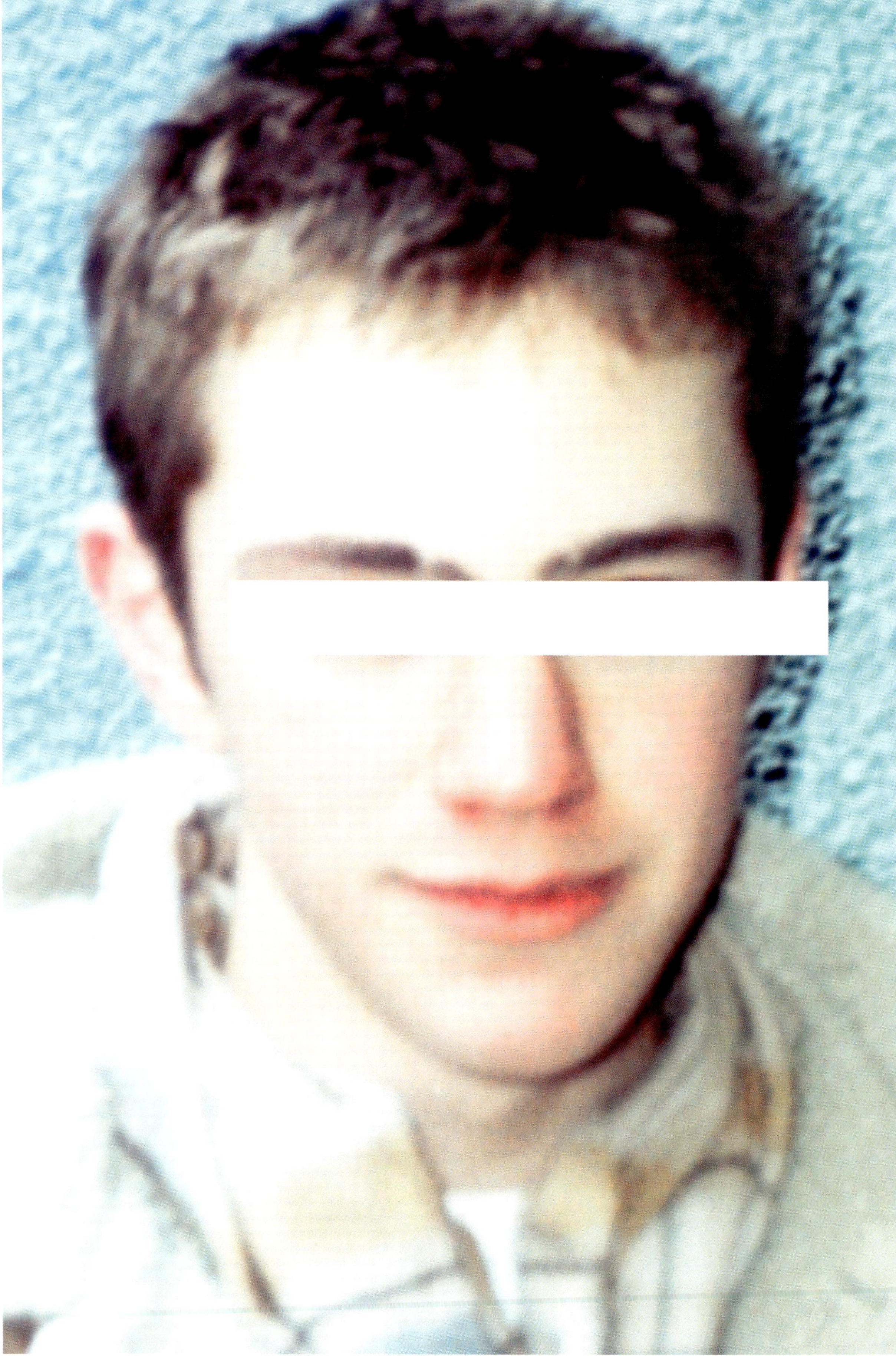

Without doubt *The Stop* is a thing. A 'We Don't Believe
You (And Even If We Did Believe You We Still Don't
Think You Should Do it)!' kind of thing.

The only problem is that *The Stop* doesn't work.
1 month after **2 million** people congregate in London
(a number so large you could be out by 50,000 and
still not be **misreporting** attendance) (and millions
more do the same in cities around the world),
George Double-yu and his zealous co-conspirators
(**us**) invade modern-day Mesopotamia, that alluvial
cradle of civilisation, anyway. Double-yu's tactic is
one of 'shock and awe'.

It doesn't take the US Army **long** to find Saddam
Hussein (autocorrect keeps changin Saddam to
Adam, and who am I to argue?). Within weeks he is
found hiding in a **hole** in the ground on a farm in the
country. It's most **undictatorial**. The US Army beat him
(obviously), rape him (all accounts opt for "sodomise"
but I'm guessing Adam did not **consent**), inspect
him for ticks and the like, then throw him in prison.
A couple of years down the line they **execute** him by
hanging. It's shown on **TV**. No news channel in the
UK shows the moment of death, *The Drop*, but they
do show him stepping onto the **gallows** and having
a thick, twisted **white** rope, noose, draped round his
neck. It lies on his shoulders. Men in **masks** do the
draping. People in the stands **jeer**. OfCom gets 30
complaints, more about the jeering than the death.
I remember watching it thinking that I'd never seen
anything like that on the news before. That was the
same *End of Something and Beginning of Something
Else,* but it was further away from *The End of the End*
and more in to *The Beginning of the Beginning.*

Everyone agrees that The *Beginning of the Beginning*
looks a lot like *The Middle Ages.*

Hardly surprising that post-the Stop (and before XR)
the protest movement languishes. The professionalised
Greenpeace/NGO side of things tick along but turn
up at a protest at any point in the 20-tens and teens,
and all you'll find is a sorry demographic that it is
both easy and **effective** to ignore: Spiral Tribe **crusties**
without a **free party** to kick you out of and **sex-pests**
claiming left wing to **cop** a feel. They will fall for
anything and, as it turns out, so will you, busy, as you
are liking and posting and adding and sexting and
unfriending then blocking and trolling and lolling as ur
viral video-world goes up in **emoji** flames.

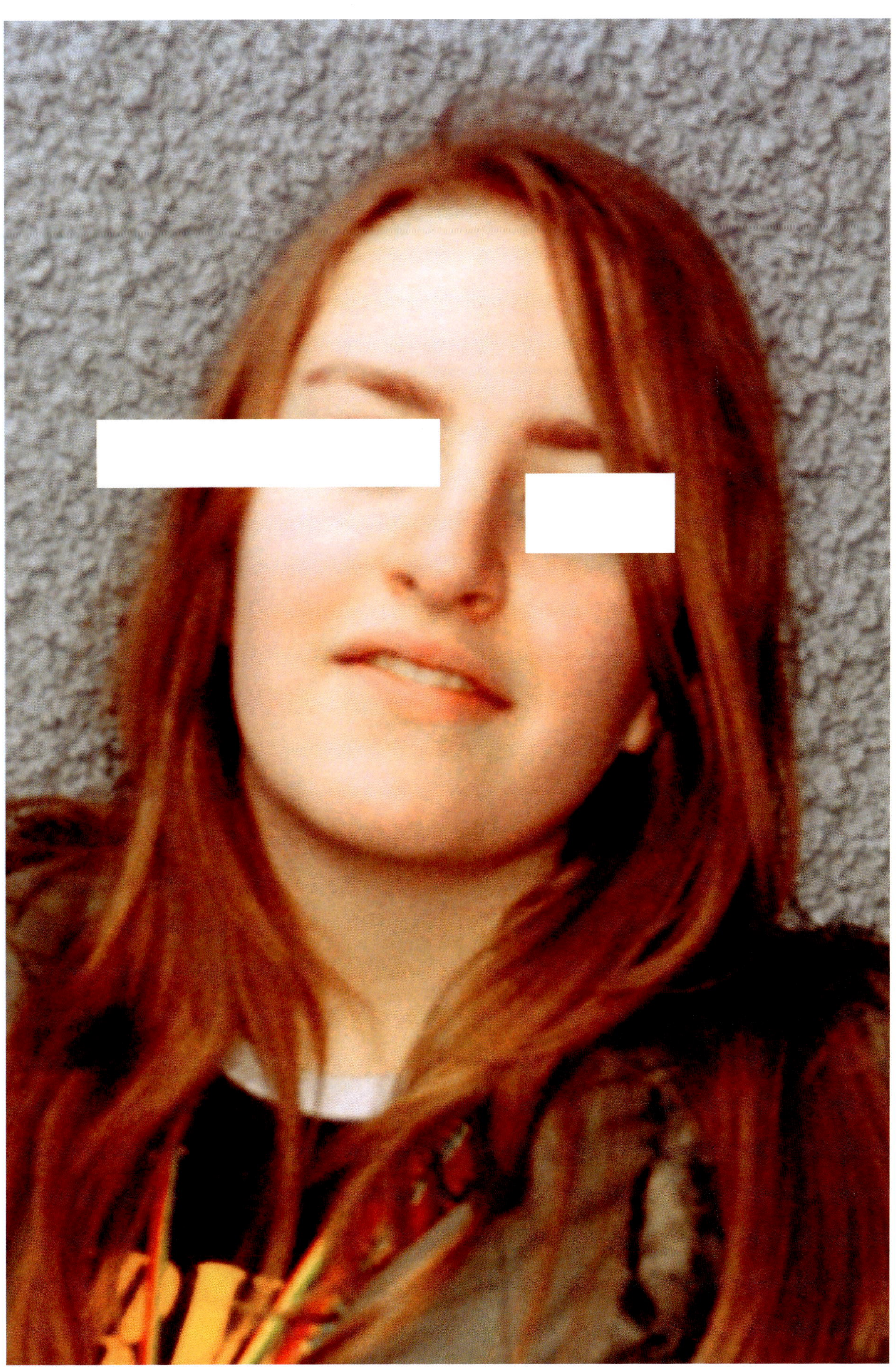

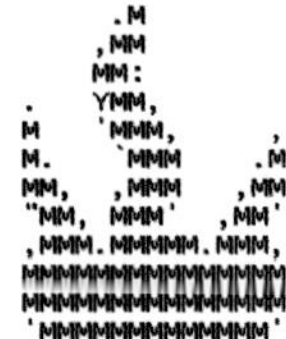

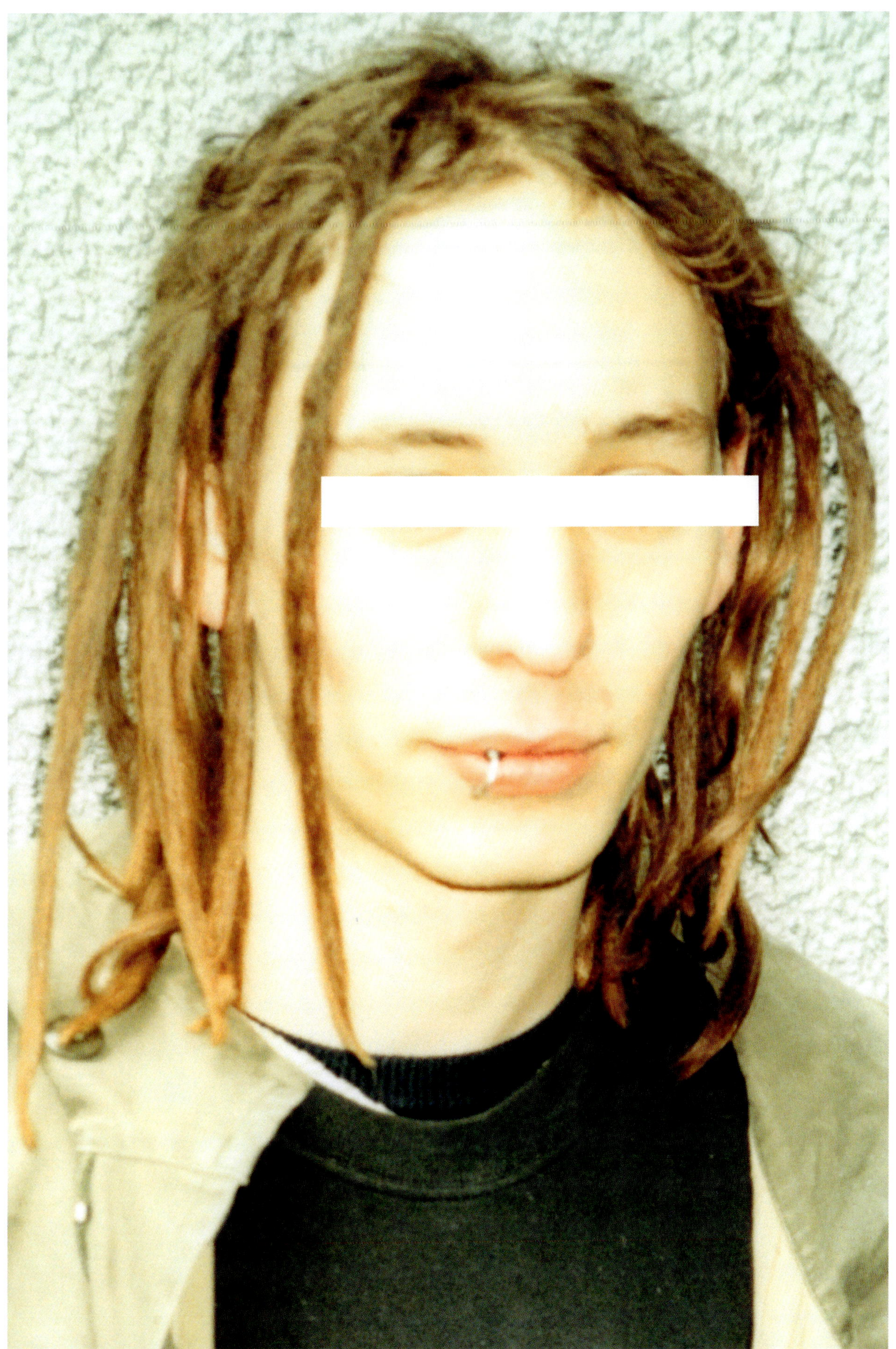

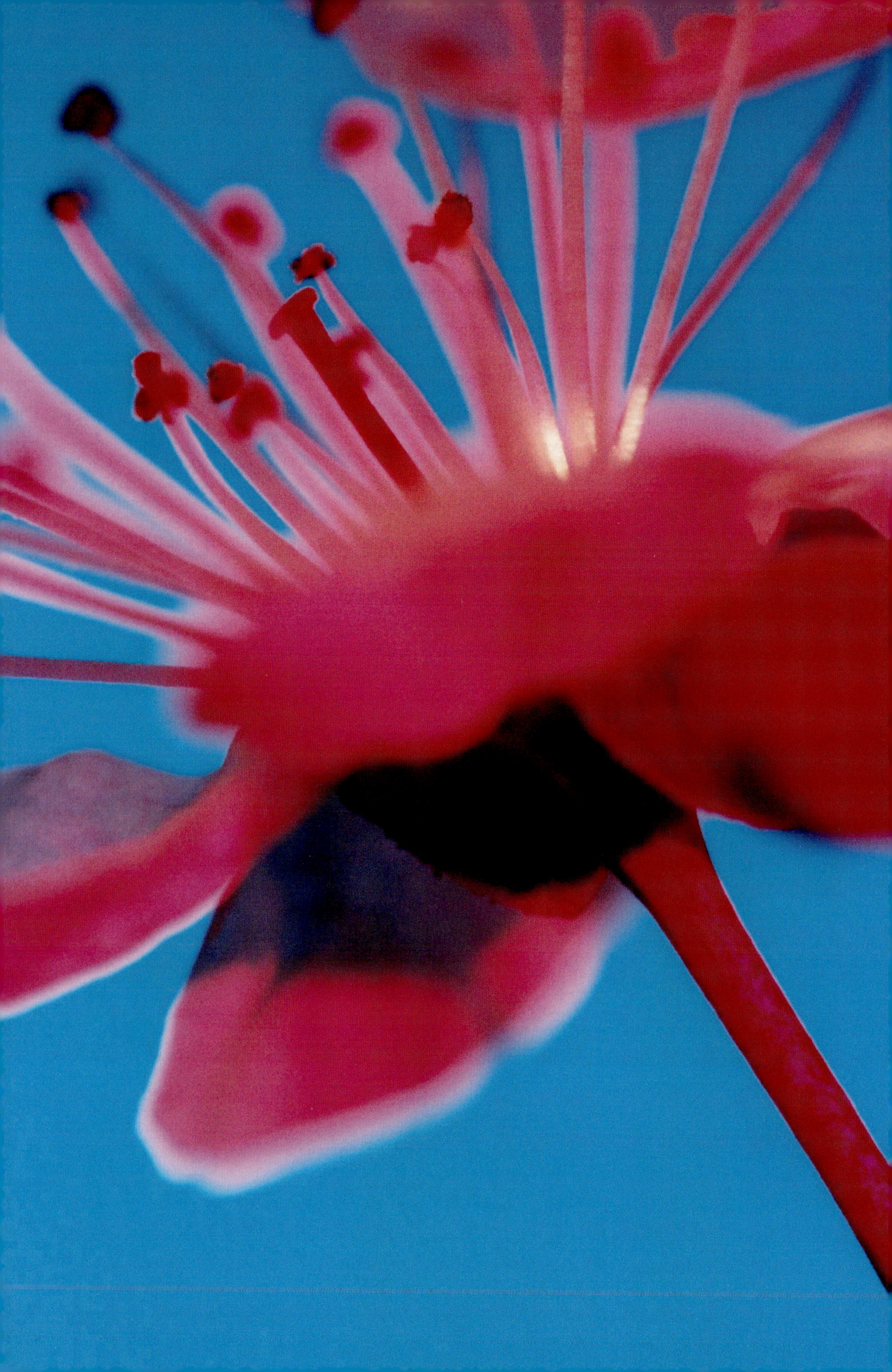

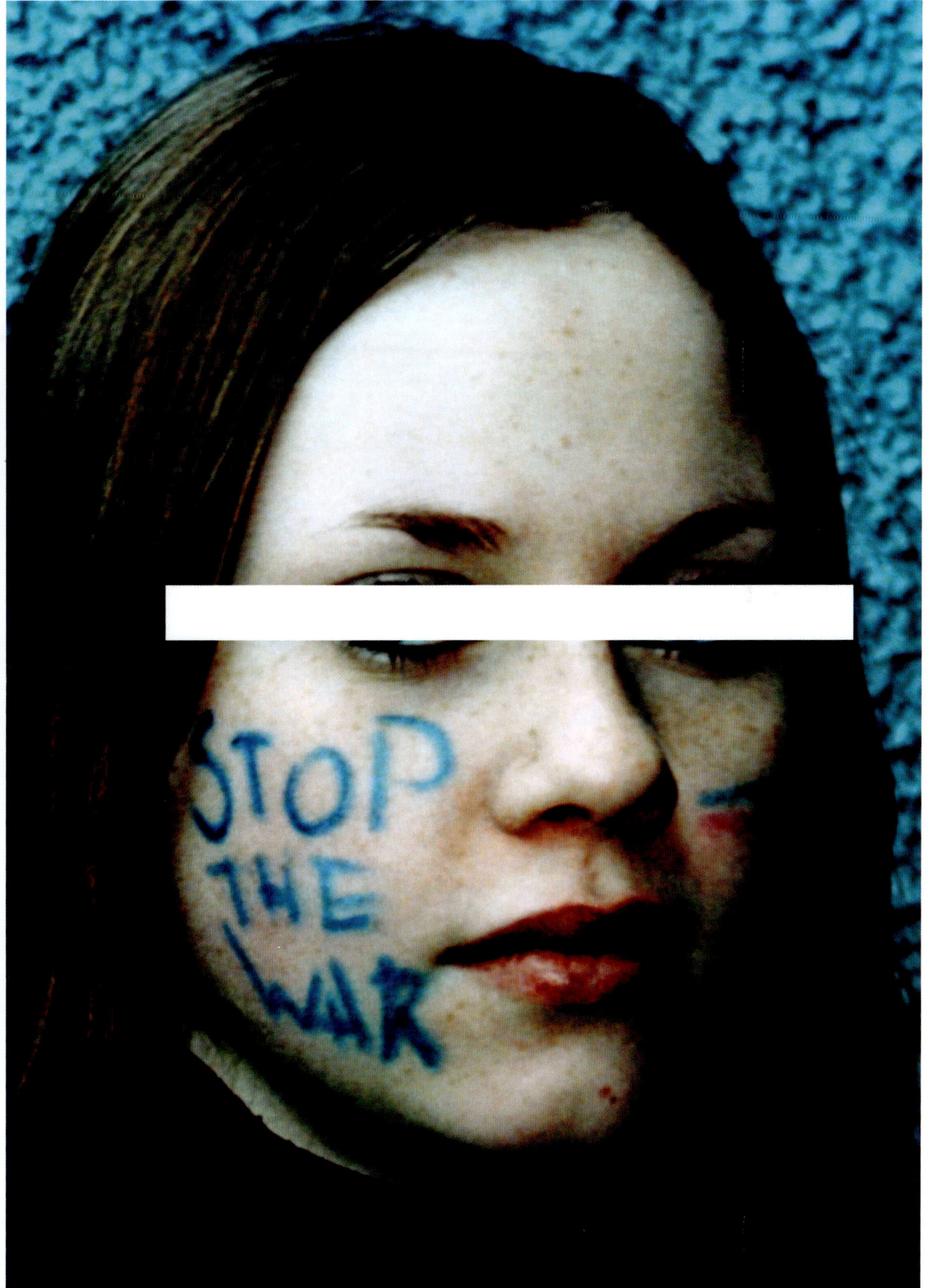

STOP
THE
WAR

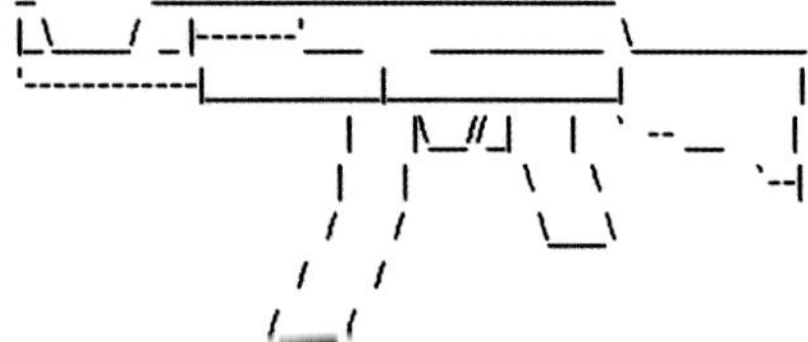

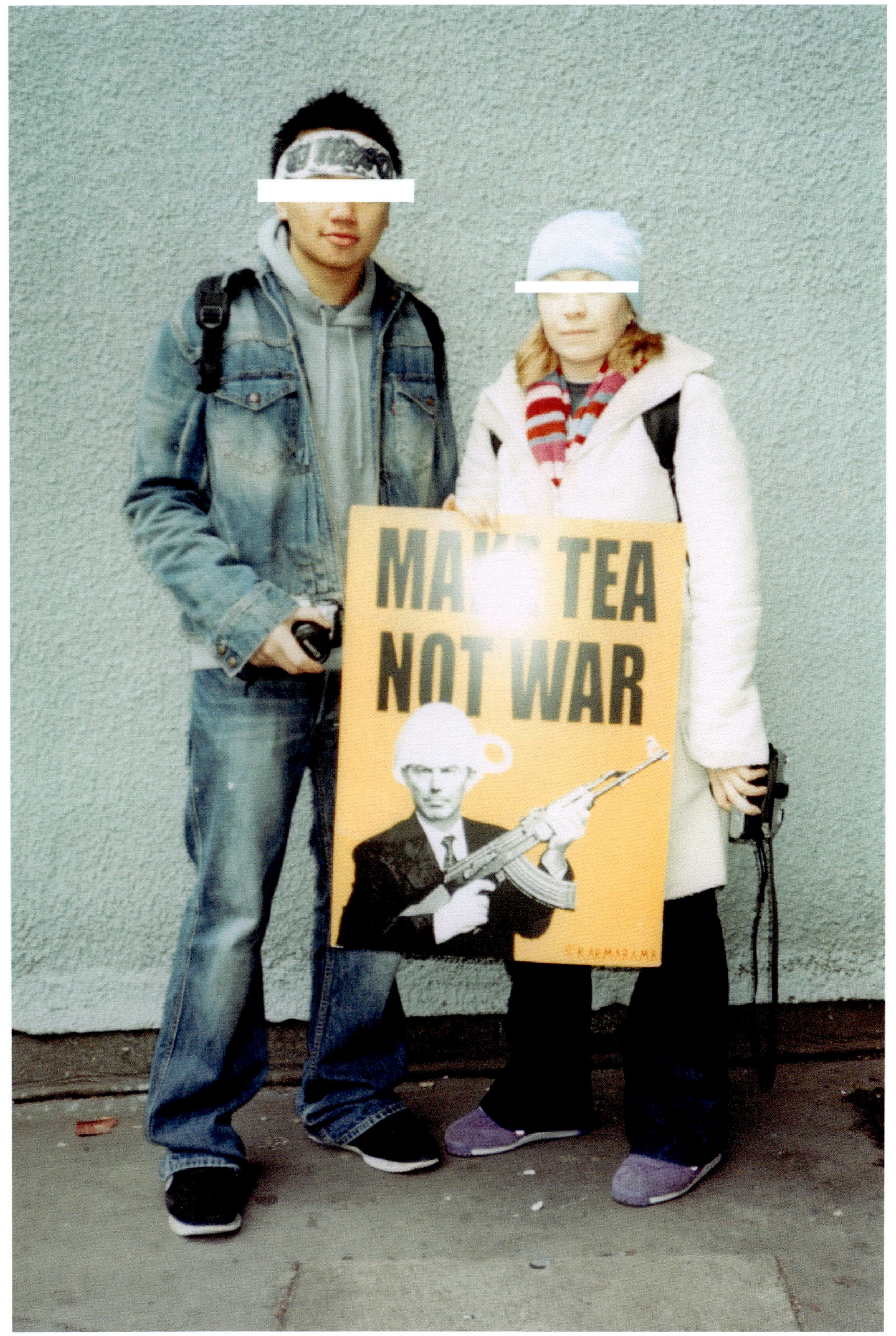
MAKE TEA
NOT WAR
KARMARAMA

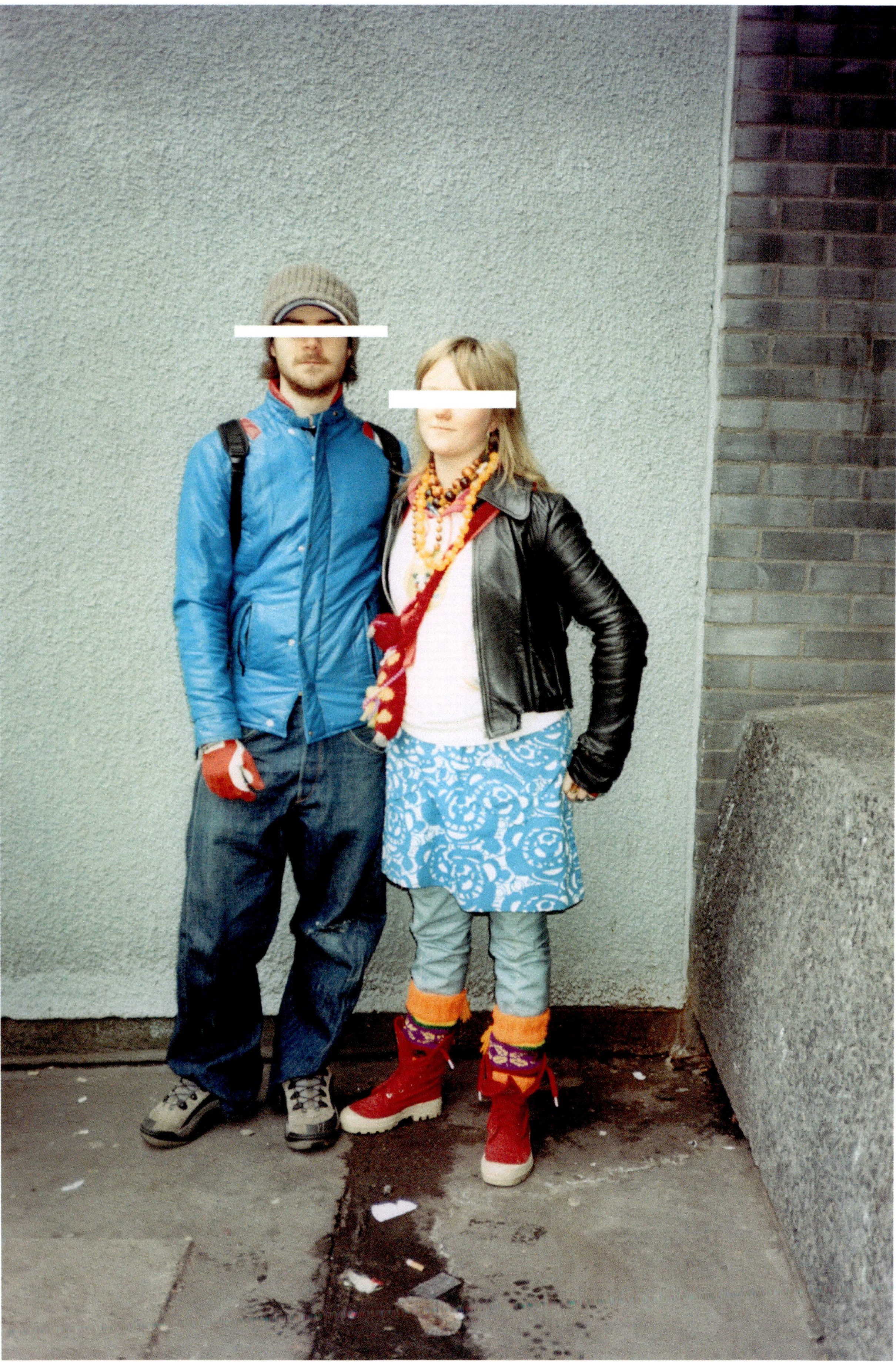

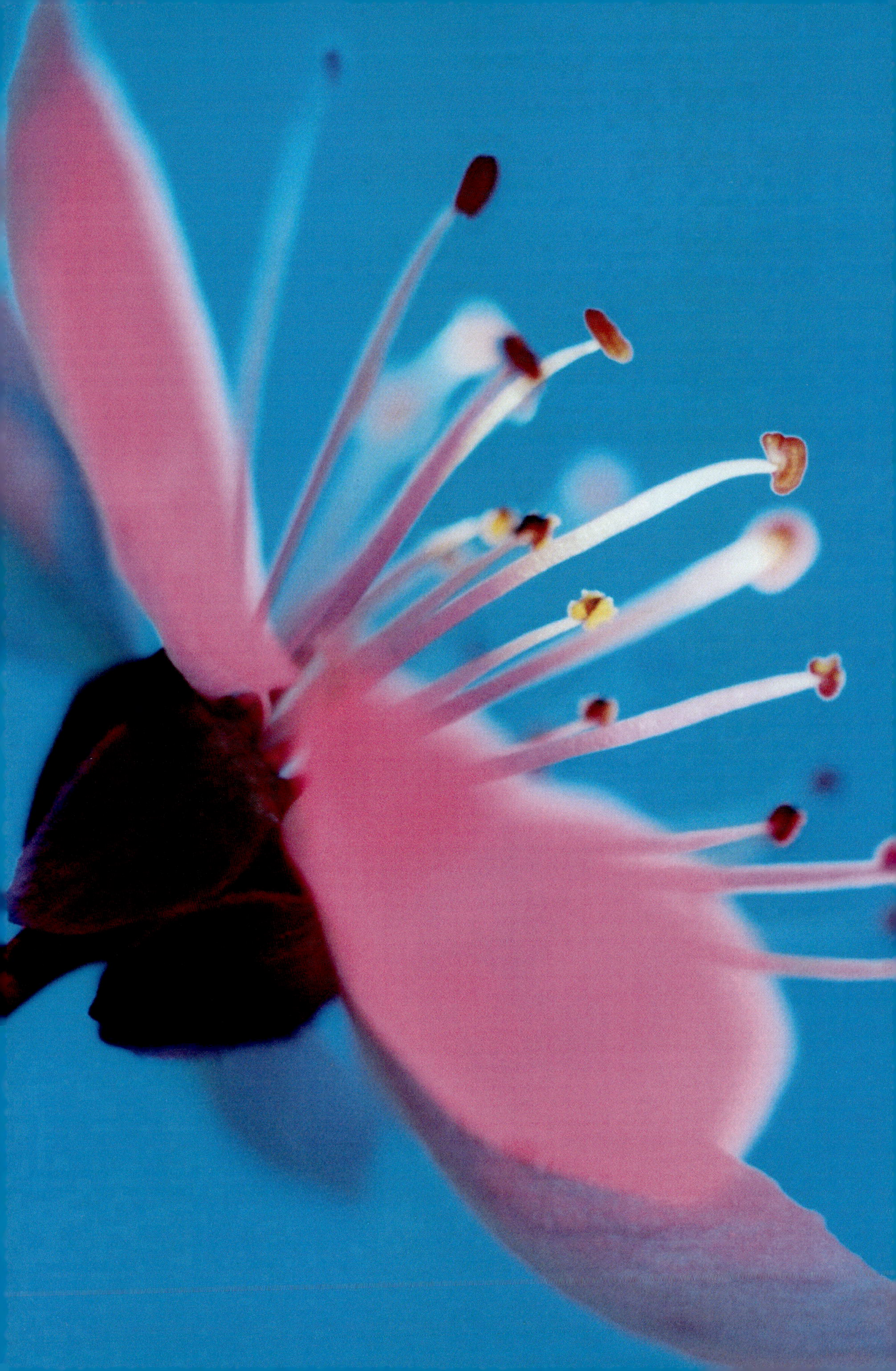

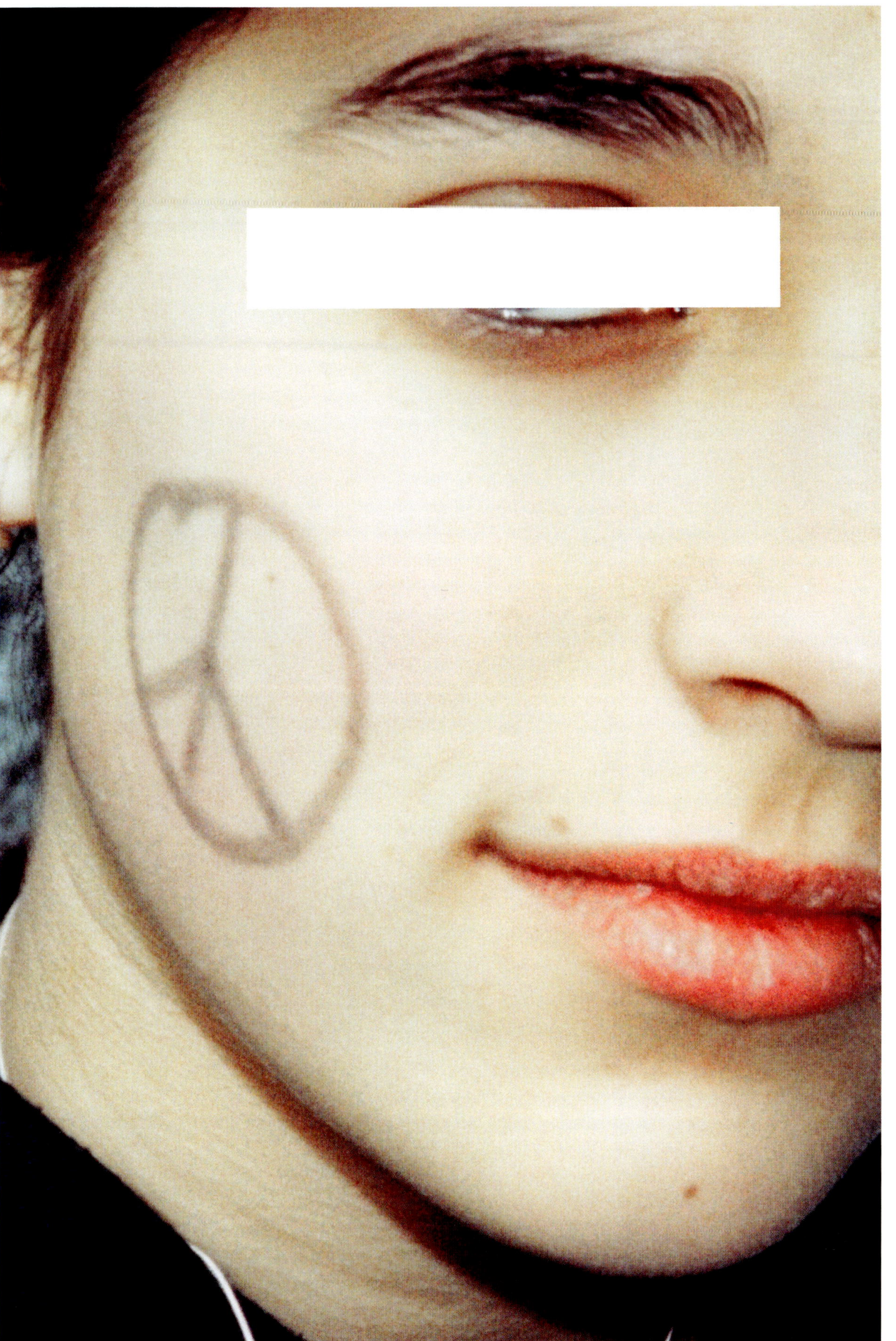

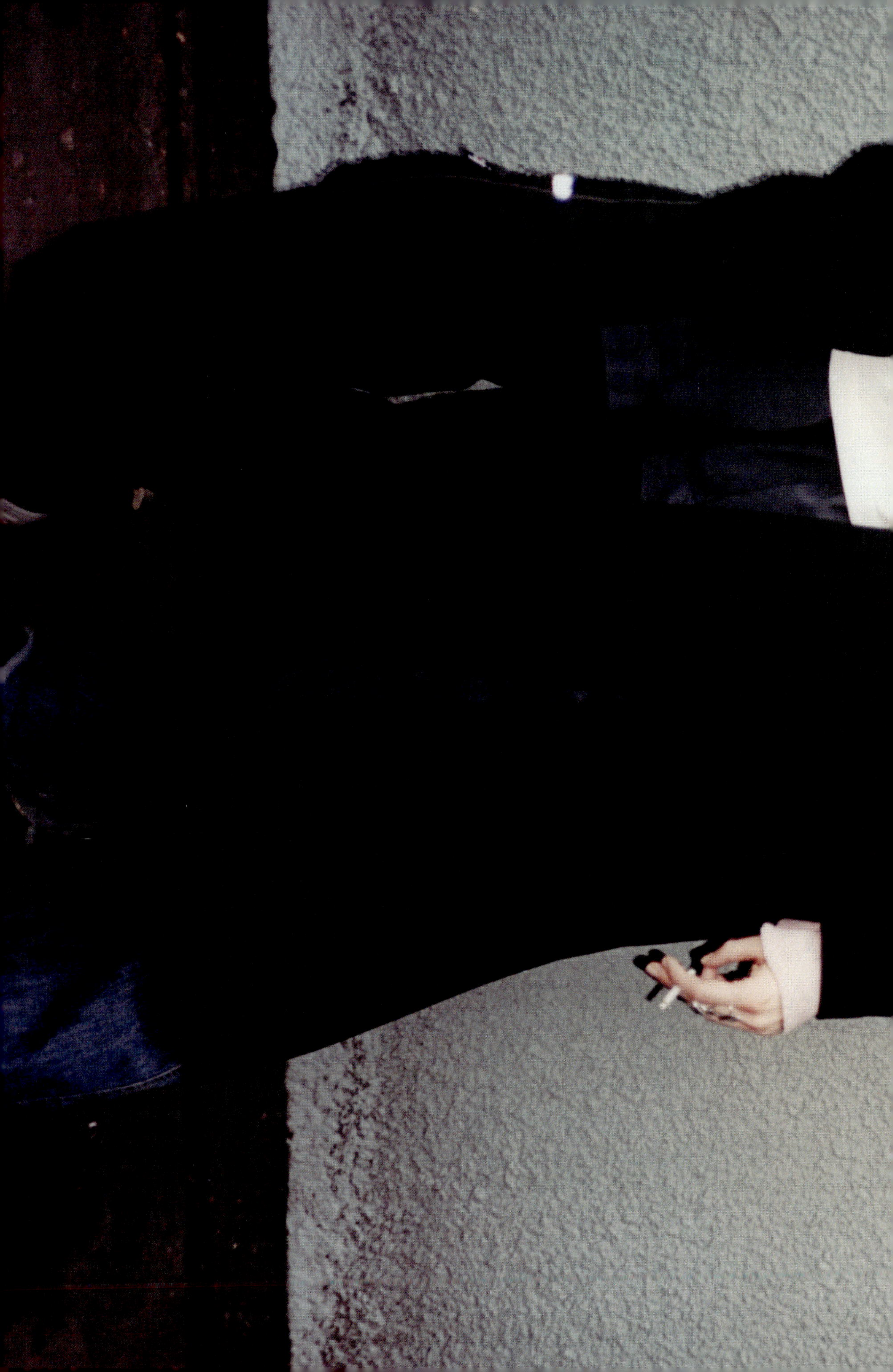

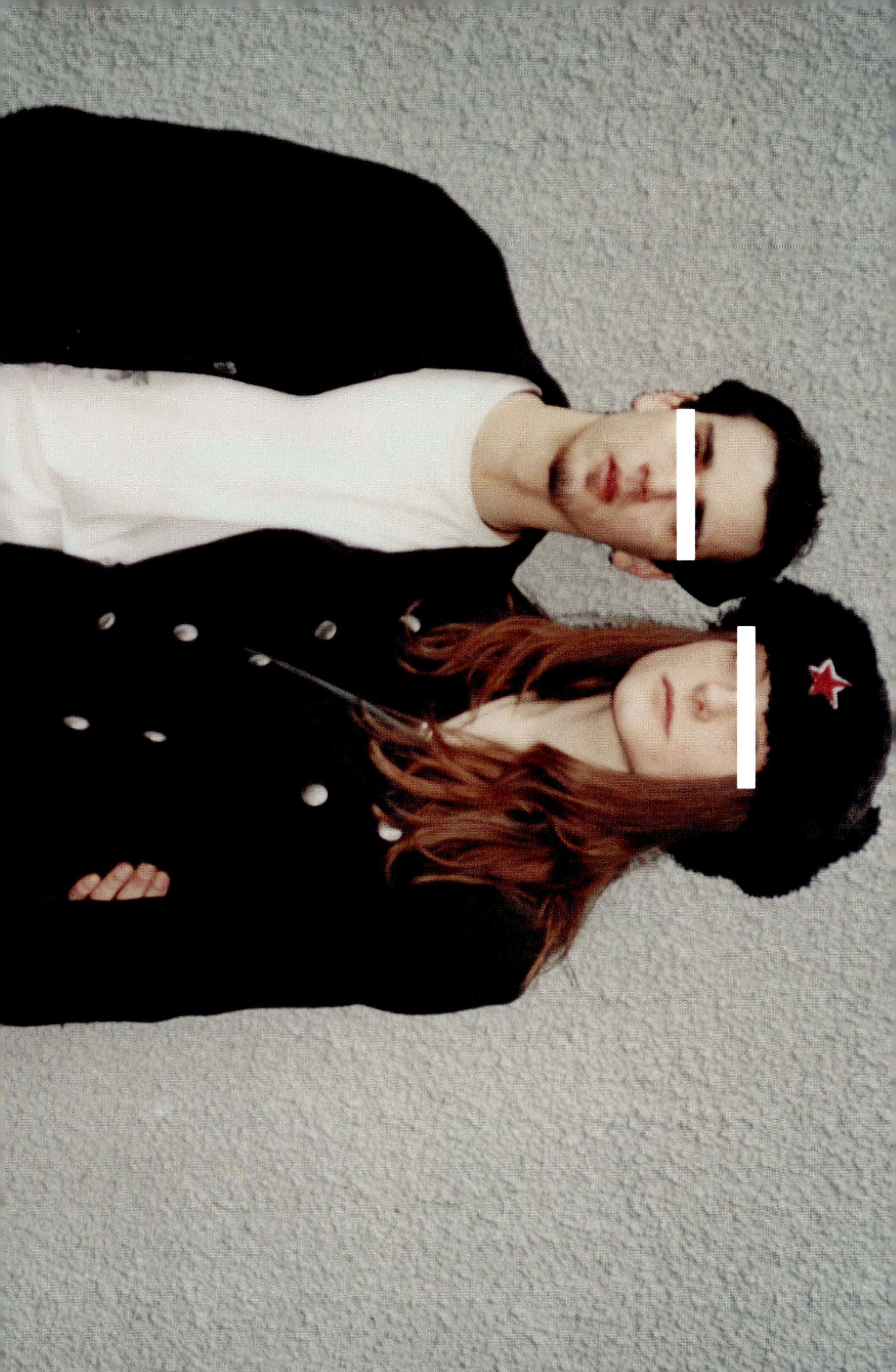

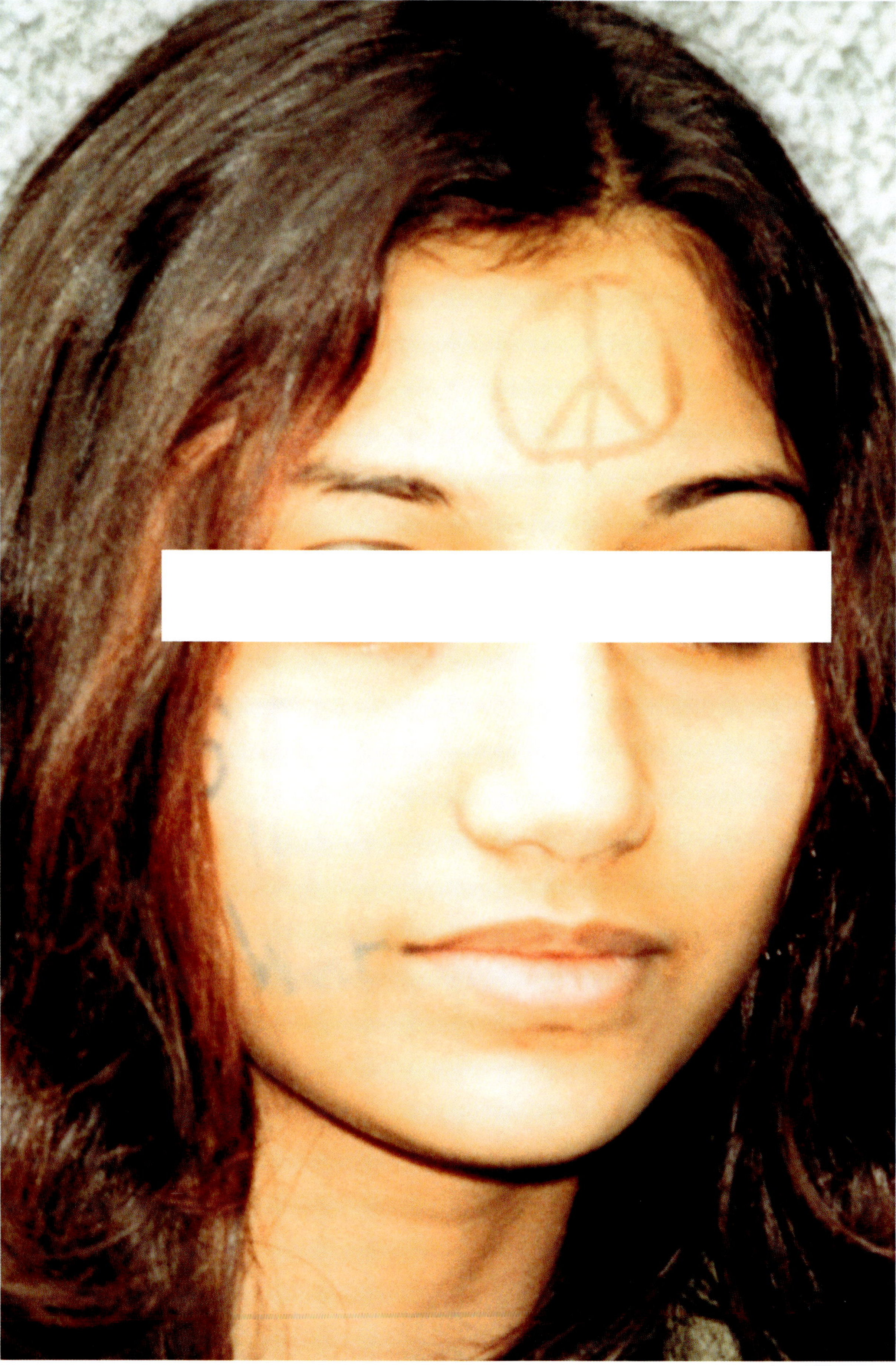

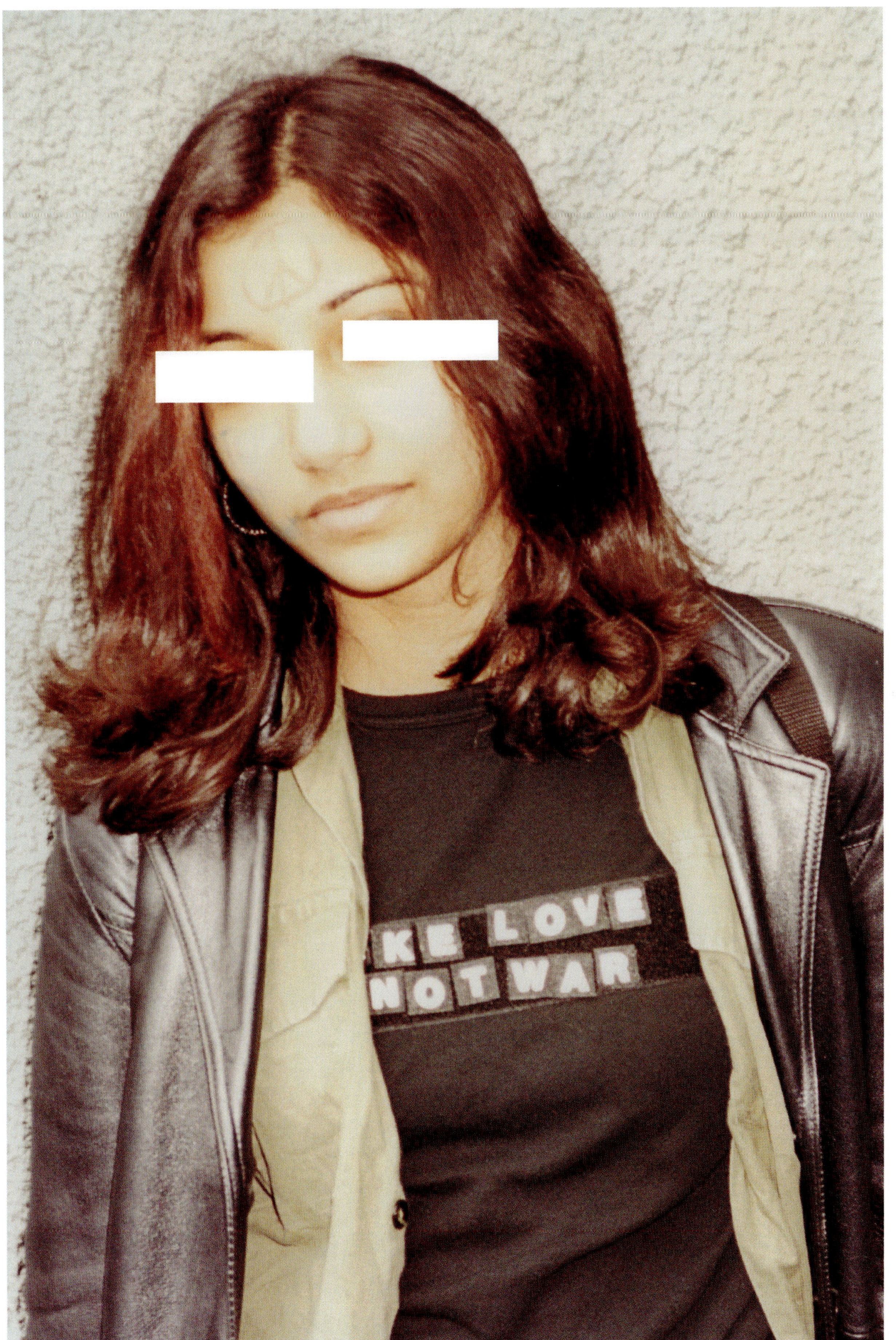
KE LOVE
NOT WAR

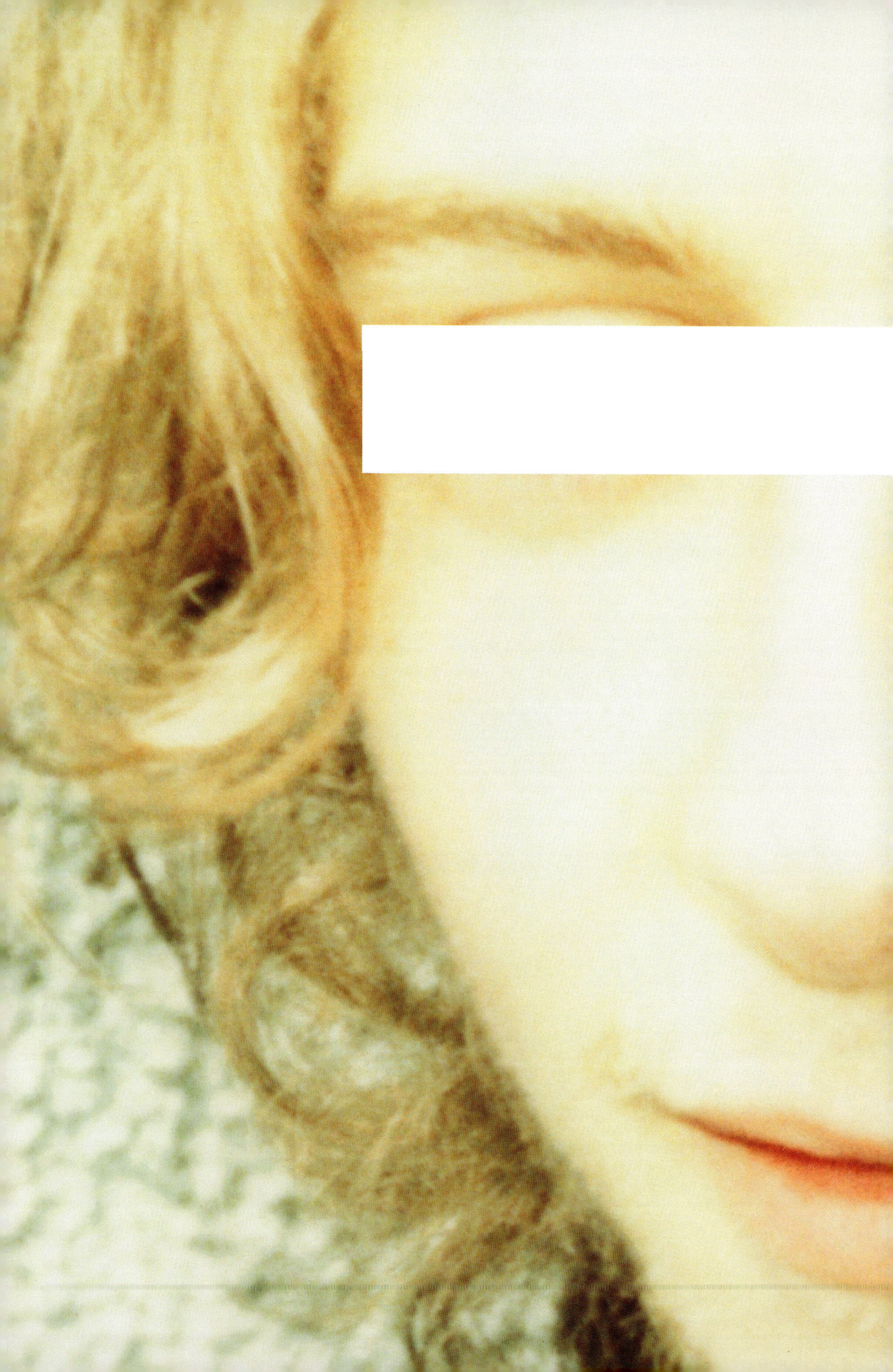

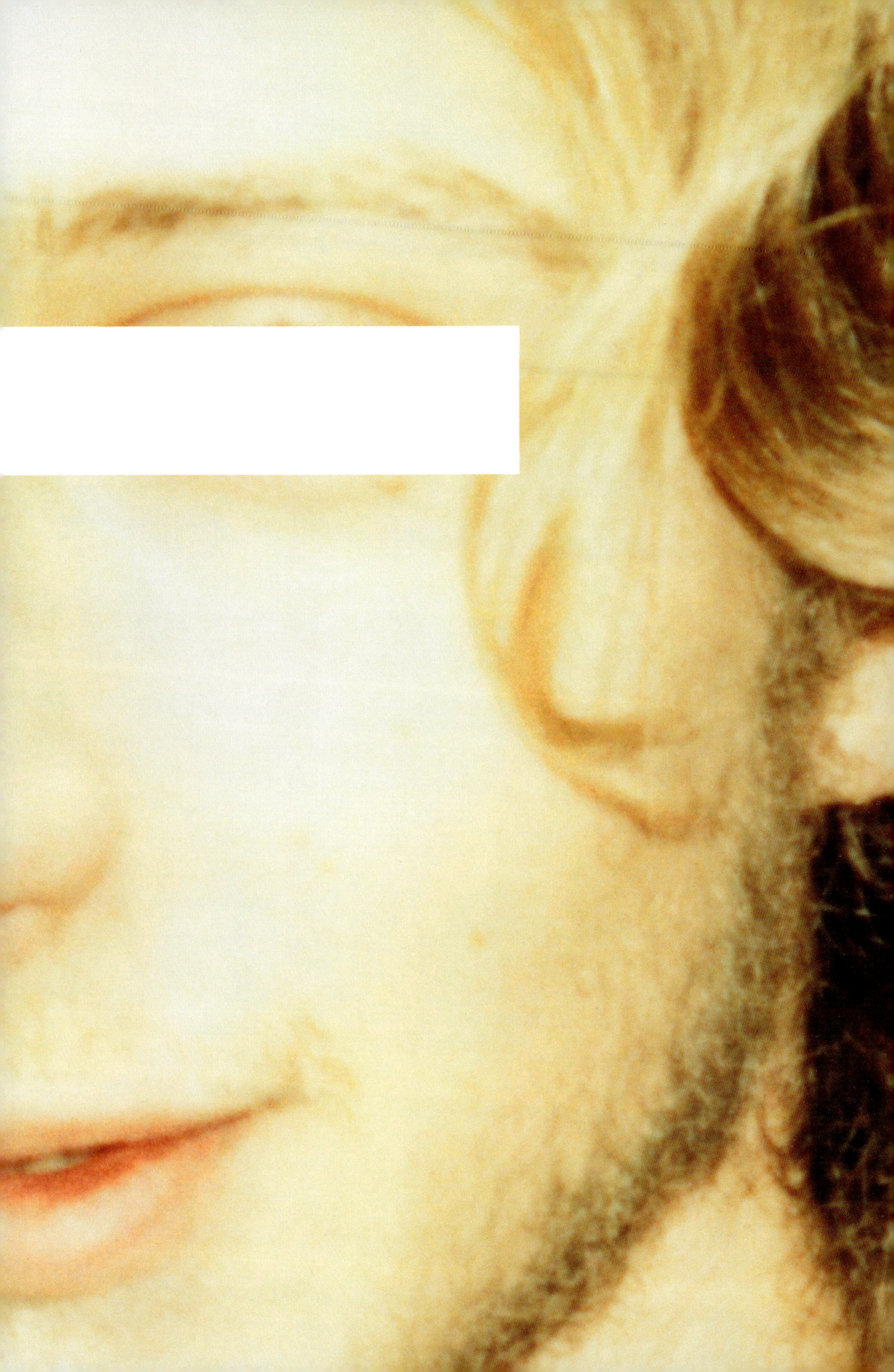

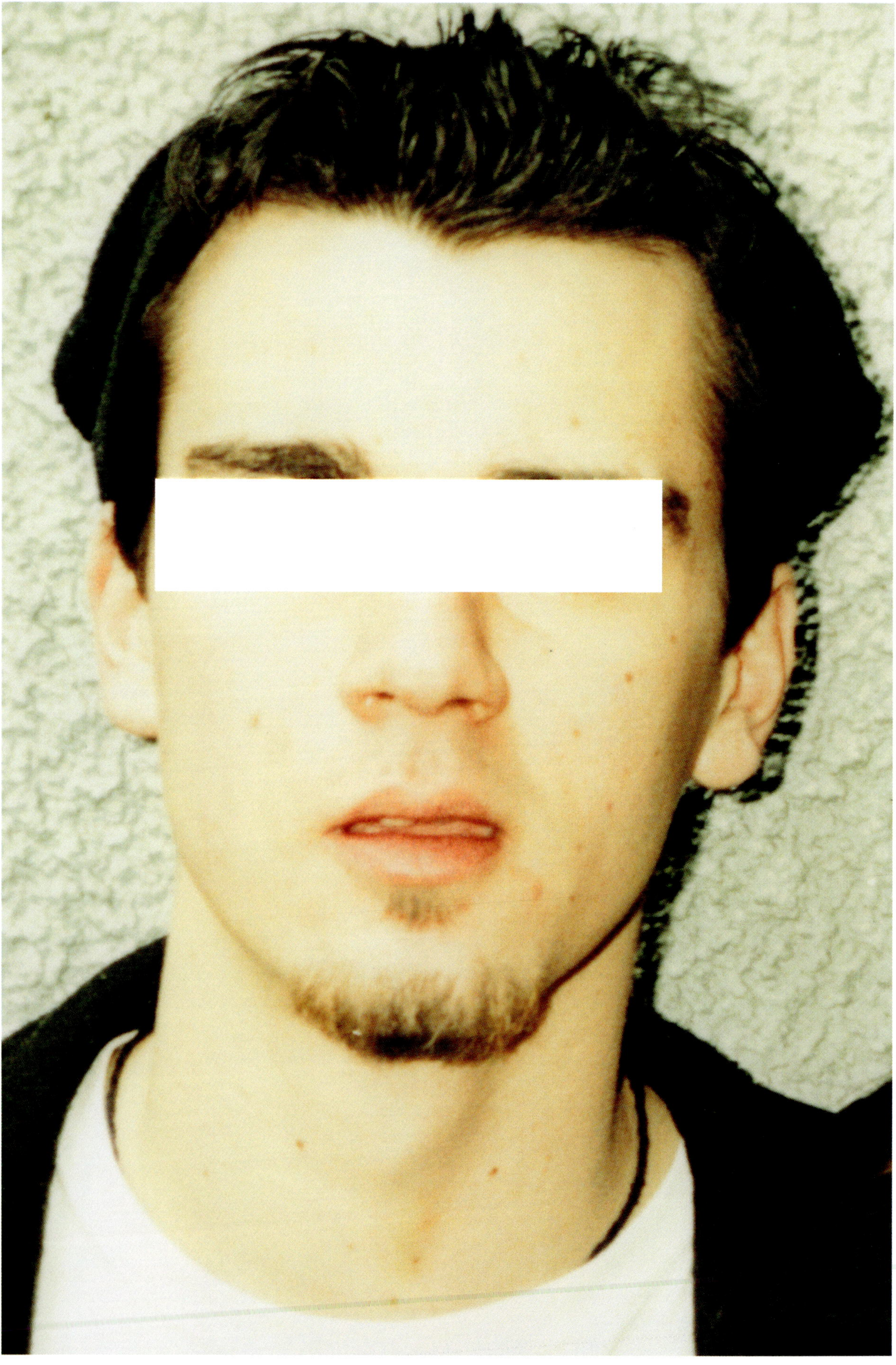

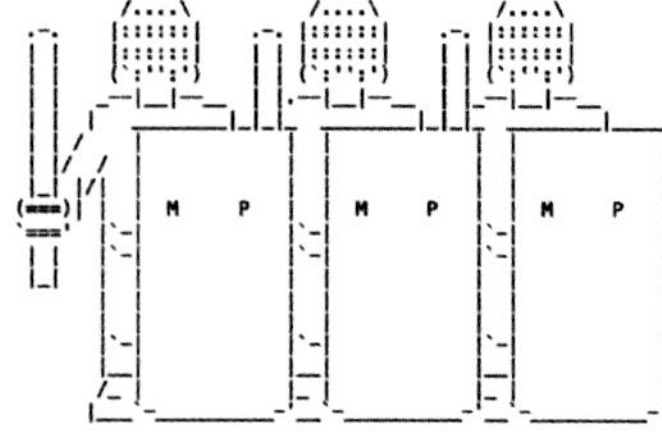

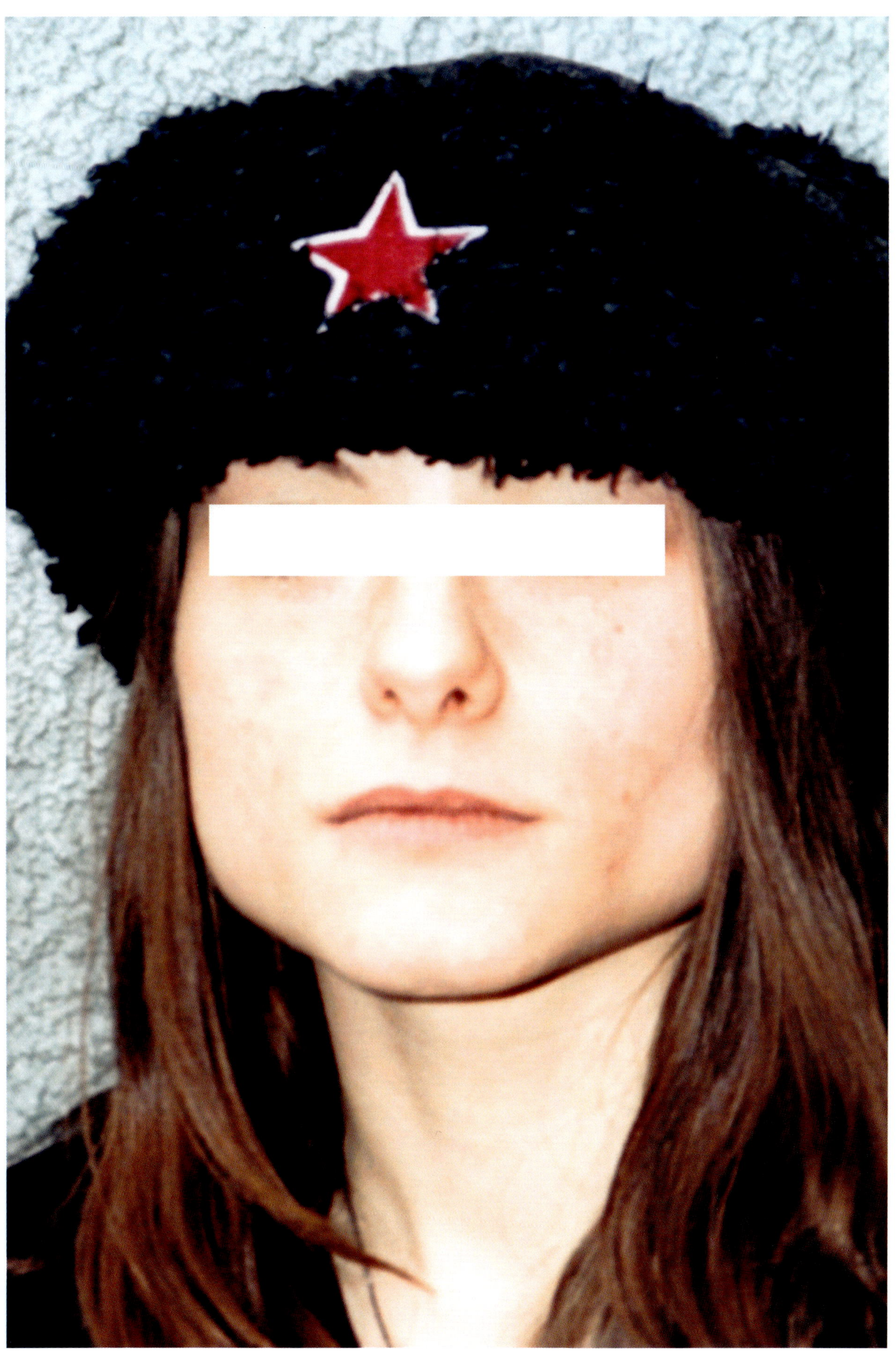

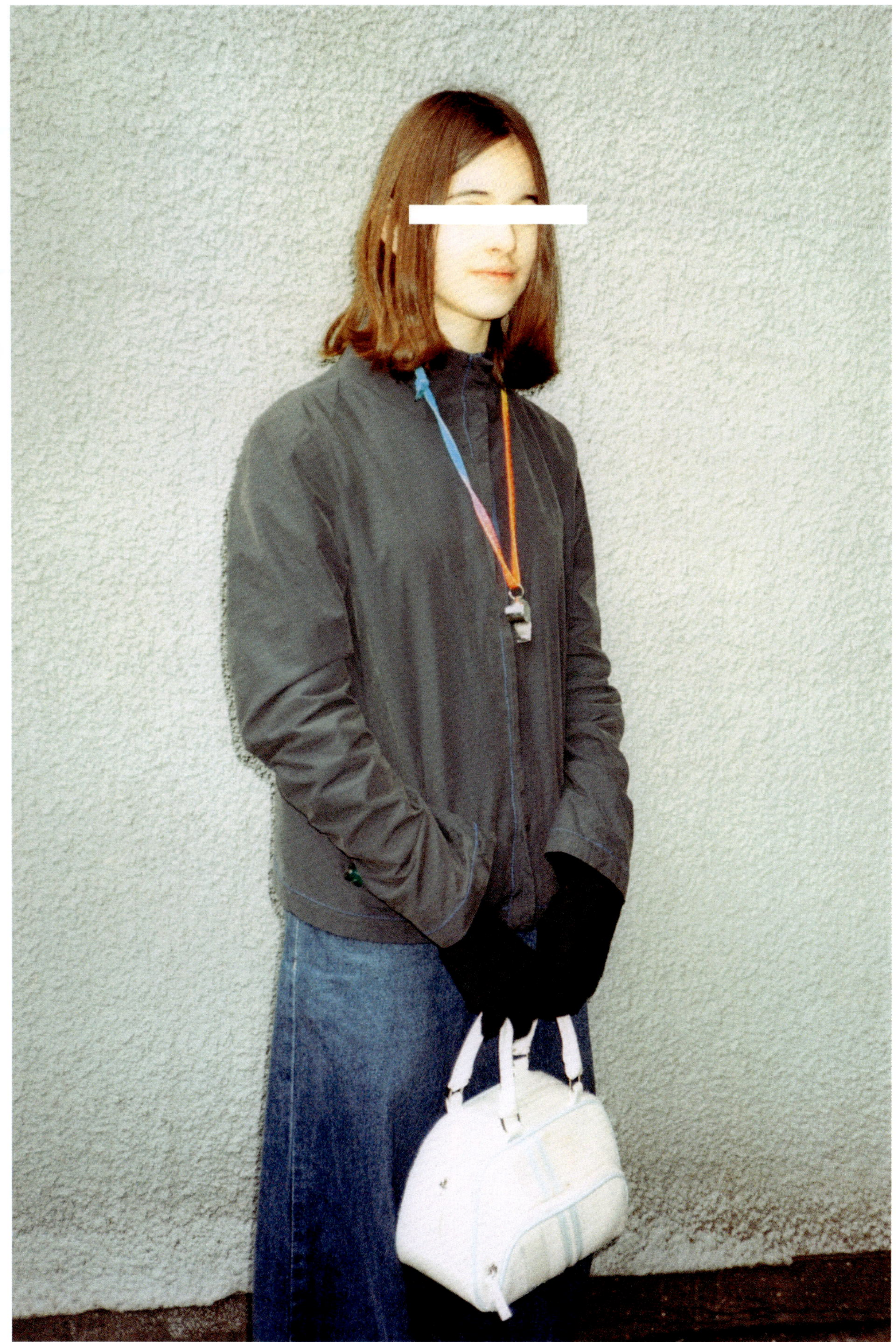

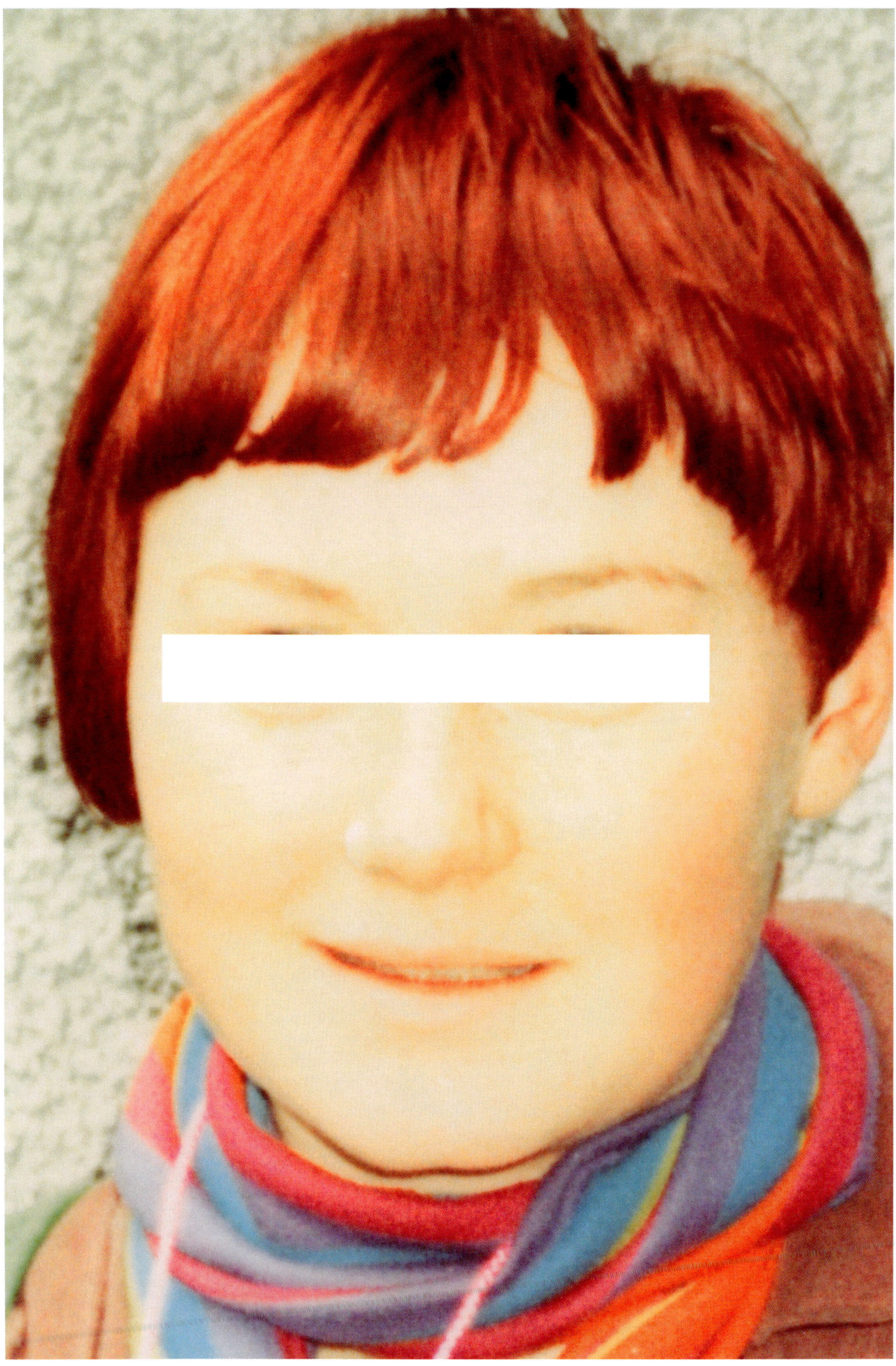

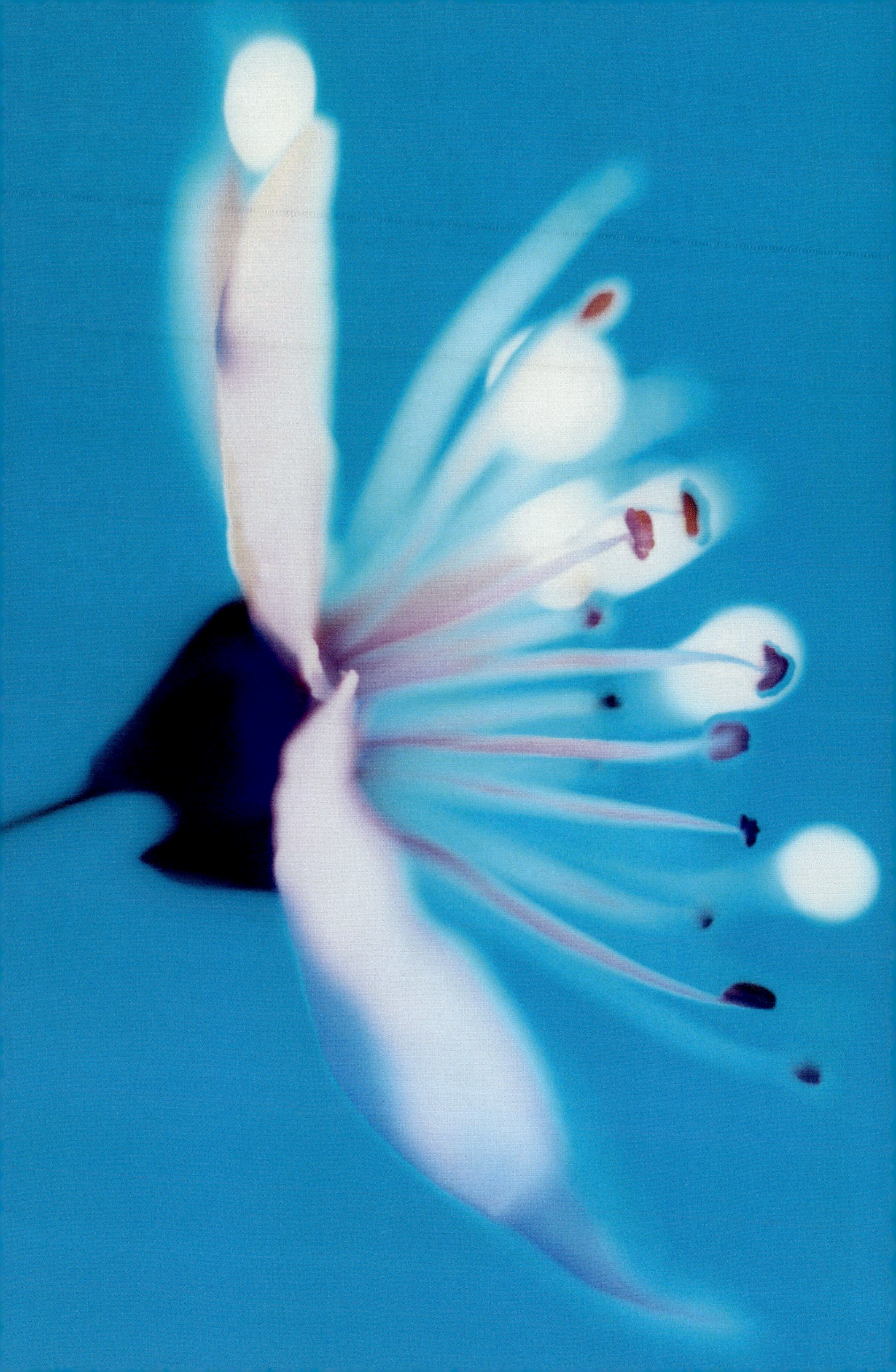

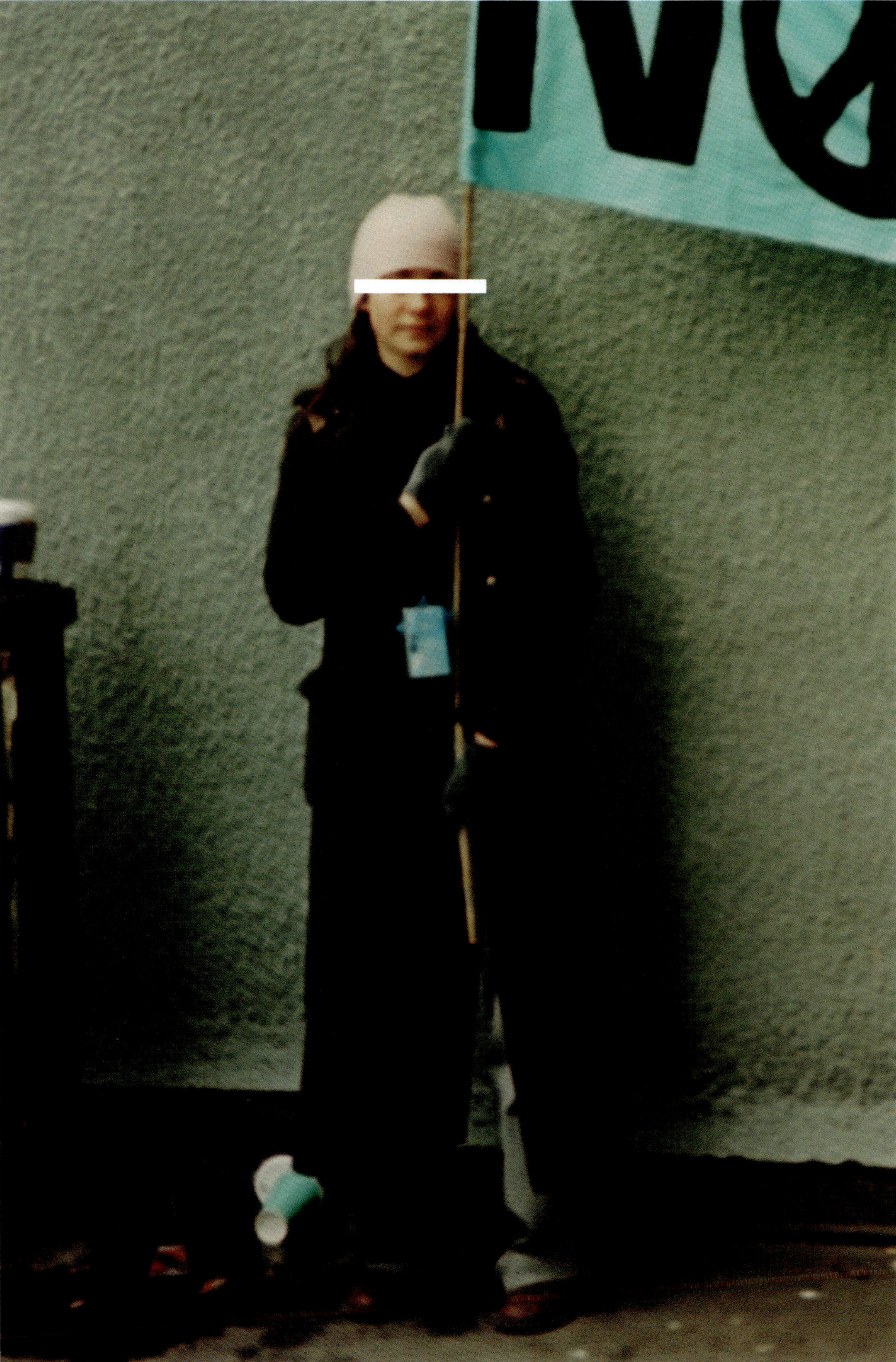

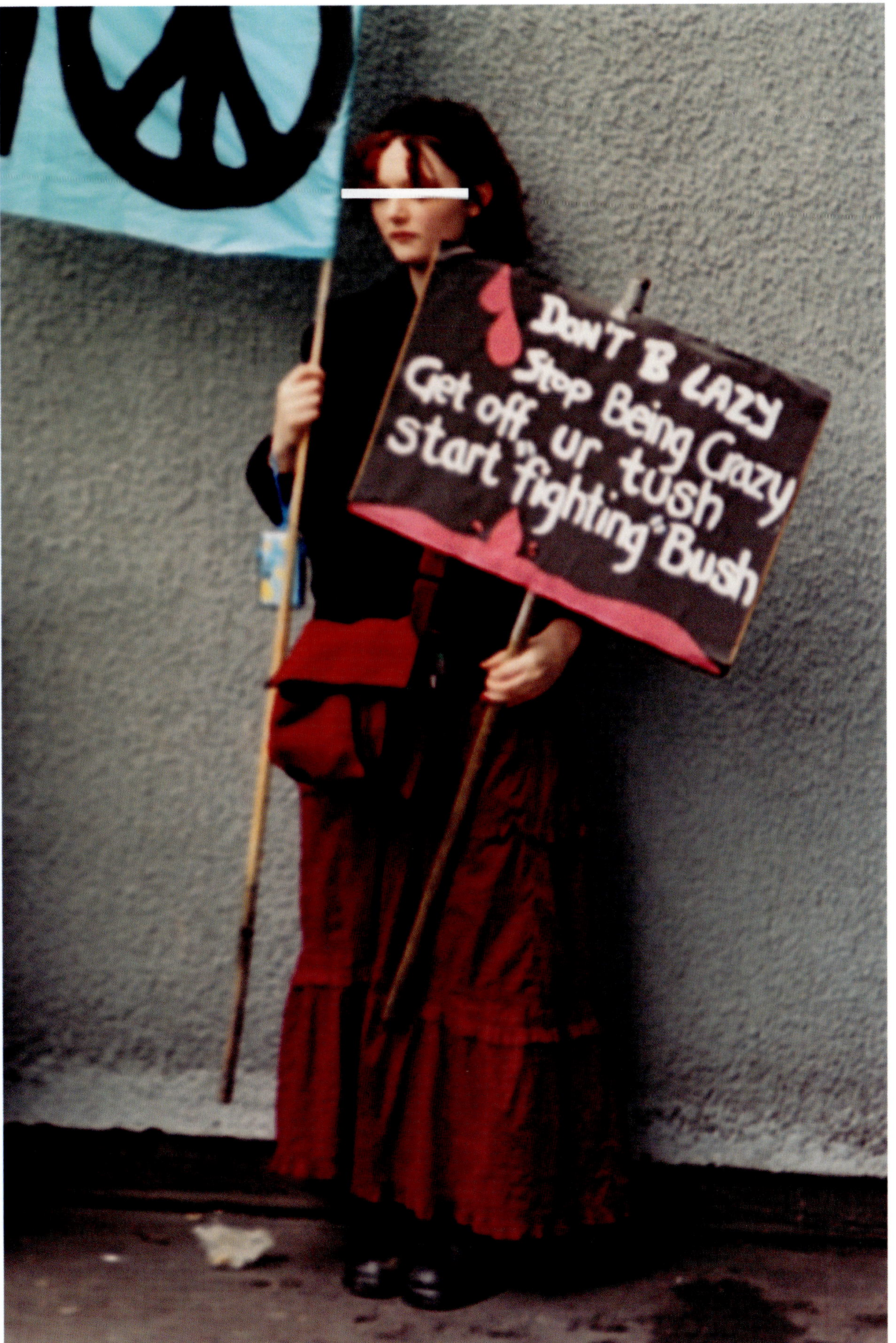
Don'T B LAZY
Stop Being Crazy
Get off ur tush
Start "fighting" Bush

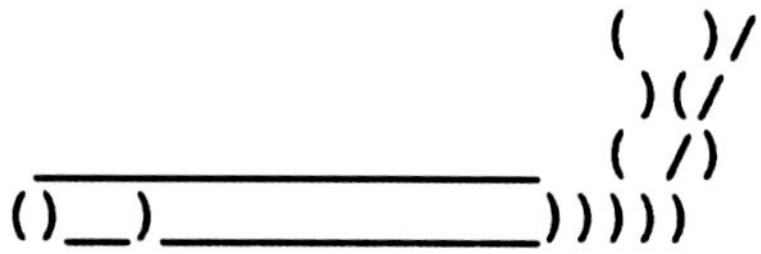

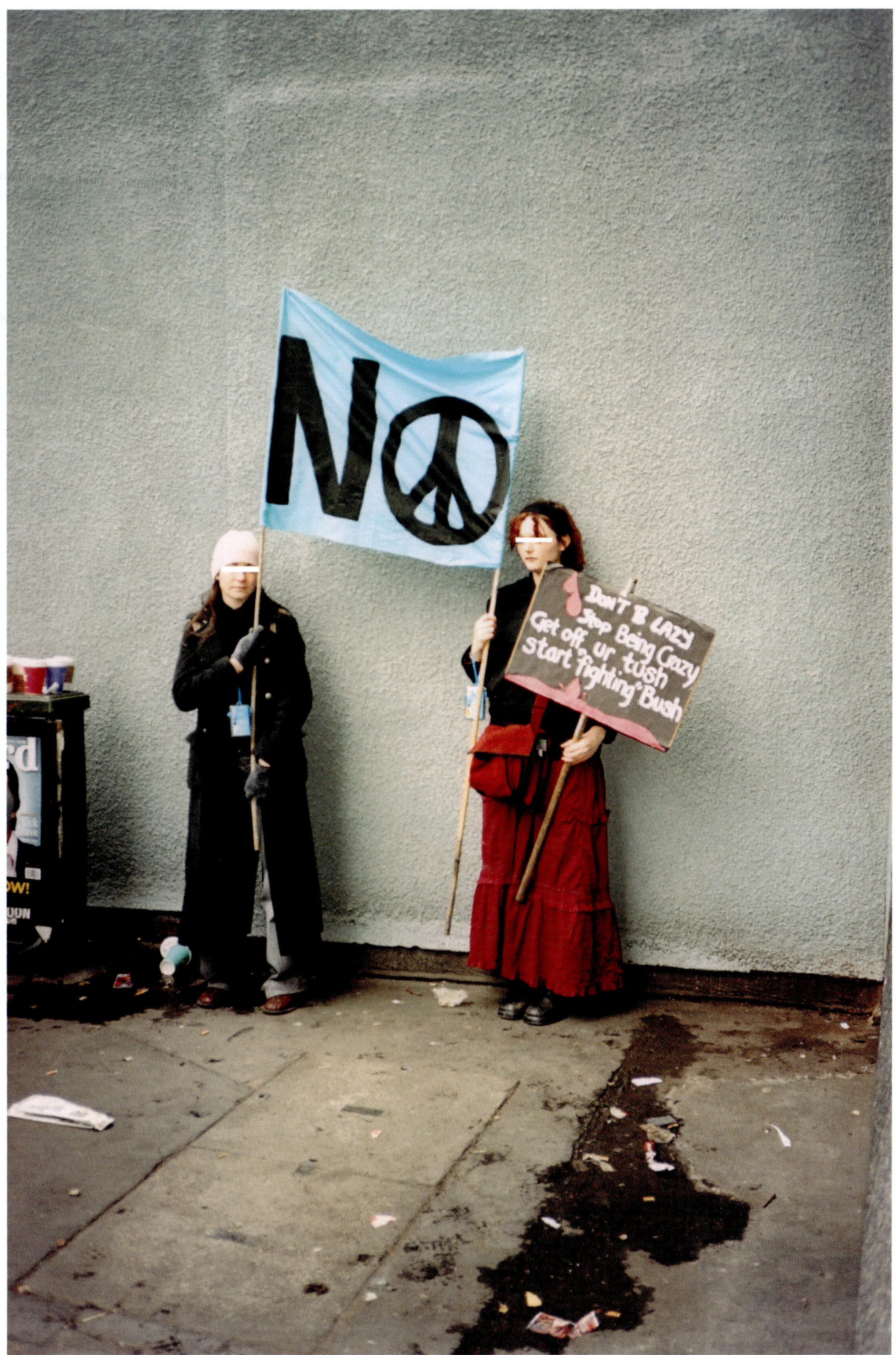

NO
Don't B LAZY
Stop Being Crazy
Get off ur tush
Start fighting Bush

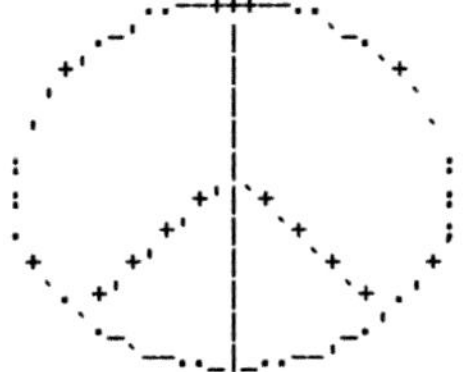

The Stop

Artwork – Gareth McConnell
Text – Iphgenia Baal
Design – Kieron Livingstone

First Edition, 2024

Published by Sorika
www.sorika.com

ISBN 978-1-7395964-5-3